HARD TIMES

BORN DIRT POOR AND ABORTION IS JUST ANOTHER WORD FOR MURDER: AND IT'S IMPOSSIBLE TO FIX STUPID !

ROBERT E. LEE ELLIOTT

KANGAROO PUBLISHING

Hard Times
Born Dirt Poor and Abortion Is Just Another Word for Murder and It's Impossible to Fix Stupid!
All Rights Reserved.
Copyright © 2020 Robert E. Lee Elliott
v2.0

The opinions expressed in this manuscript are solely the opinions of the author and do not represent the opinions or thoughts of the publisher. The author has represented and warranted full ownership and/or legal right to publish all the materials in this book.

This book may not be reproduced, transmitted, or stored in whole or in part by any means, including graphic, electronic, or mechanical without the express written consent of the publisher except in the case of brief quotations embodied in critical articles and reviews.

Kangaroo Publishing

ISBN: 978-0-578-22600-2

Cover Photo © 2020 www.gettyimages.com. All rights reserved - used with permission.

PRINTED IN THE UNITED STATES OF AMERICA

Table of Contents

This book is divided into four sections

(1) Dedication i
(2) Foreword iii
(3) Introduction..vii
(4) Story.. 1

Dedication

This book is dedicated to the hard working dirt poor scratching just to survive with an unshakable belief that that the meek shall inherit the earth.

That goodness and mercy will rain down upon the children of God and right will always prevail over evil.

Foreword

Unless a person has experienced a life of being poor and without they will never understand what it means to exist in a life of poverty. Being ripped off and taken advantage of by the system called Due Process is nothing new to a poor man. Whether the so called elite likes it or not the poor people are the backbone of America. History has shown that the poor people built, defended and made America a great country admired by the rest of the world.

America is a nation of laws which has been taken to the extreme in far too many cases. The country is completely over run by lawyers who know no boundaries when it comes to filing lawsuits against anyone. I personally have had lawsuits filed against me based entirely on perjury and accepted by judges knowing that the affidavits were being filed under perjury. At present the law profession with lawyers has become nothing more then a band of well dressed thieves with a license to steal.

They have gone completely over the top when filing civil cases. Any person is taking a calculated risk if he or she happens to fart on a crowded elevator and a lawyer happens to be a passenger on the elevator. You can rest assured that a lawsuit will probably be filed against you and everyone on the elevator will be subpoenaed as a witness against you including the Environmental Protection Agency.

Book writing is a piece of cake because it's easy to explore your mind and thoughts but having it published and sold on the market is something else to behold. Anytime you turn on the television to Fox News you will probably see one of the host or guest showing a book that he or she has just written. One guest was showing a book that his wife had just written regarding some short stories and he said that he had 10,000 copies printed and they were sold out in two weeks. I suspect that him saying he sold 10,000 copies in two weeks is nothing but a lot of bullshit.

A poor slob like myself has to spend hundreds of dollars to advertise their book on Amazon or Barnes and Noble. The television host and guest gets to advertise their books dozens of times to a national audience free of charge and within a week or so they say that it's a New York Times best seller. Hell, in my book writing adventure I'd be thrilled to sell ten books much less 10,000. It would be nice to have your book placed in a book store for shoppers to see but there doesn't seem to be a way a poor man can get it done without taking a second mortgage out on his house.

If you don't remember anything else, please remember this. We're all born ignorant but some people work real hard to be stupid and it's impossible to fix stupid. Once you've accomplished becoming stupid you're stuck with it for the rest of your life. Stupidity knows no boundaries and it can run in the people that you least suspect including family members. A man can be intelligent as hell and his brother may be as dumb as a rock and the biggest asshole in town. No one is immune from having asshole friends and family members.

The primary topic of this book will be devoted to the author's life so you can begin to understand the trials of the dirt poor and a life of hard times and how easily your life can be destroyed by our imperfect justice system.

All of the writing is based on the opinions and experiences of the author and deals with non fiction. I have no interest in make believe and creating make believe people. Rules for writing is nonsense to me and if I think someone is an asshole I'll call him one.

Introduction

This book will basically relate to the author's life and the trials and tribulations that he endured to survive. The dirt poor, homeless and sick will be able to understand his life.

On occasion it will be pointed out how America is slowly becoming a third world country. For instance right now there are thousands of people from shit hole countries in Central America at our Southern border with Mexico threatening to crash our border wall to enter America whether we like it or not. At present it is estimated that our country has 30 million illegal immigrants or 10% of our population and they're still pouring in by the thousands. Whether you agree or not but in my opinion the business world caused the entire influx of immigrants because they wanted cheap labor. Between the baby squirters, the chicken shit young men and criminal element, they present a national security problem for America that the Socialist Democratic Party refuses to acknowledge.

The Democratic Socialist House of Representatives will be chaired by a flaming ass moron that thinks that the idiot Al Sharpton has saved America. She exposed her level of intelligence when she stated before congress "Let's pass the bill so we can find out what's in it."

Regarding the little skinny peek squeak Al Sharpton, I first met him in the 60's when I threw his fat ass out of the police station in Miami,

Florida for causing a disturbance. At the time he was a fat ass with long hair and a mustache. As he grew in life as a sheep herder claiming to be a preacher to a "no justice, no peace" racist, he became a close advisor to President Obama visiting the White House 176 times during the Obama administration. Apparently he rained on the parade of hairlip Jesse Jackson because he seems to have dropped out of the picture. My goodness where is poor Jesse these day?

To have a better understanding where I'm coming from you should know that I hold an Associate of Arts Degree from Miami Dade Community College, a Bachelor's Degree in Criminal Justice from Florida International University and a Master of Science Degree in Administration from Biscayne College also located in Miami, Florida. In addition to the various degrees I also served 25 years in law enforcement with the Dade County Sheriffs Office in Miami, Florida. My military background consist of 8 years in the United States Naval Reserve which I hold an Honorable Discharge.

I will take you through my life from childhood to manhood so you can understand what it means to be a nobody fighting to be a somebody. Anyone with a pen and piece of paper can write about being poor but living it is something else. Sometimes life doesn't seem to be fair especially in the area of advertising a book or whatever else you're trying to sell. In my particular case I have to pay through my nose to place any kind of advertisement. It appears that almost everyone on Fox and Friends has written a book and they constantly show and advertise their books on national television free of cost. In desperation I contacted one popular individual that has a radio show and he wanted $6,000.00 a minute to advertise my book on his radio show. That's just an example of why I think life can be unfair.

As for myself I don't write make believe and fiction. All my writings are based on my true life experiences and personal opinions, not make believe characters and stories. You will see that I have absolutely no love or respect for lawyers and judges because both are cut from the same cloth. After years of confronting lawyers I'm totally convinced that most are nothing but well dressed thieves with a license to steal and being a judge indicates how good you were at it. They can rob and steal and don't even have to wear a mask or have a gun which is just another example of life being unfair. Hell, John Dillinger, Jesse James and Bonnie and Clyde couldn't hold a candle next to a couple lawyers when it comes to robbery.

The last two judges that were involved in a lawsuit against me were so inept neither could hit themselves on their ass with a bow fiddle. One couldn't give a shit and the other one placed more importance on a piece of ass then justice. The lying female lawyer that continually sued me over a period of 20 years was either one hell of a muff diver or a fantastic blowjob because she could get any circuit court judge in the county to sign anything even after being told that the affidavit was based solely on perjury. I suppose that I shouldn't be too critical because the judge is only human and enjoys a nice blowjob like everyone else.

Well, enough of who I am and how much I've been kicked around, let's get to the story.

Story

Whenever I write I only relate to my life experiences and express my own personal opinions. My writings are for the common people and can be easily understood. Fiction literature has never appealed to me because make believe people and stories doesn't contribute anything to a person's intelligence. Everything will be in plain simple language eliminating the need for a dictionary. In addition to normal and average people my writings can also be understood by lawyers, judges and other mentally handicapped people.

Follow me through a life of hard times and begin to understand what it means to be dirt poor and living in poverty. I was born on October 19, 1934 in Beaverton, Alabama which was a pathetic little country town that was nothing more than a wide spot on the highway. The biggest industry there was growing cotton and making whiskey. When my mother gave birth to me she was assisted by the old country doctor that had never attended any kind of medical school or had any formal training regarding medical procedures. He was recognized by everyone in town as a medical doctor because he was the only one in town that seemed to know what he was doing in an emergency. I was fortunate to have him attending my birth because I was born with the umbilical cord wrapped around my neck choking me. I was called a blue baby because my color had changed due to the lack of oxygen. The doctor kept submerging me in a large pan of water until I started to cry and breathe.

HARD TIMES

All of my brothers and sisters were born in the same bed in the same old house. An old broken down two story house that looked like it would fall down in the slightest wind. It had no indoor plumbing, running water or electricity for lights or heating. There was no such thing as a refrigerator or electric stove. Having an indoor restroom was unheard of and every house would have an outhouse someplace nearby. Toilet paper usually consisted of a Sears Roebuck catalog and most of the outhouses were equipped with two holers in case two people had to go at the same time. At night each house would have a slop jar available which was kept underneath a bed in case someone had to have a bowel movement.

At night you'd have to carry a kerosene lamp around with you in order to see where you were walking. In the Winter time everyone would have to gather around the fireplace to keep warm. There was no such thing as a telephone and I had never heard of such a thing like a television set. The first time I ever even saw a telephone was when we moved to Miami, Florida. I couldn't wrap my mind around to actually being able to talk on a telephone.

Every now and then I always offer my readers a tid bit of information to make their life easier to accept and it will certainly make you smarter. For instance if you're not banging your spouse then rest assured someone else is.

When we were living in Alabama and had a storm approaching my mother would take all of us to the storm shelter in case our old house fell down. The storm shelter was a cave that my dad had dug into a large bank next to the highway in front of our house. He installed a large wooden door to keep us safe. We would stay in the shelter all night long with some blankets and a kerosene lamp. During the night as I laid on a bench trying to sleep I could hear the large wooden door shaking and rattling all night long from the high wind. I'll never forget how the wind would shake the door and make me wonder if our old house was still standing.

Even to this day every time I hear the song "Polk Salad Annie" by Elvis Pressley, it reminds me of the hard times my family endured to survive. Sometimes I have to laugh my ass off when I hear young people of today bitching and complaining how hard they have it. They have never known hard times and to be without even the necessities of life. It's a job trying to get a kid to mow the lawn much less hoe a ten acre field of corn or pick cotton in the hot sun all day long. If they don't get an allowance, wear designer clothes and have a car to drive around town, they feel like they're being cheated out of life.

When I was growing up on our farm my mother made my clothes out of empty flour sacks and store bought clothes were unheard of. As I grew older I only wore hand me down clothes from my older brothers and was glad to get them.

One of the happiest days of my life was when my oldest brother brought two little puppies home with him. We named them Left and Right. At Christmas time my older brothers would go into the woods and cut us a Christmas tree. We never decorated the tree with lights because we didn't have electricity in the house. My older sisters would hang some bulbs on the tree and anything else they could find to make the tree look pretty. The only thing that we would exchange at Christmas morning was our love for each other because our family didn't have the luxury of money for buying gifts. My mother had an old broken down piano that she had gotten from her mother and I'll always remember how she'd play a song entitled "Red Wing, Beautiful Red Wing." She would sing and play the piano as we all would sit around her. Christmas morning was a thing to behold in our family. We didn't have toys or pretty gifts to enjoy but that didn't matter because we had each others love. I would give everything I own If I could only be in that circle one more time and hear my mother sing.

HARD TIMES

At my young age I still believed in Santa Claus and as I laid in bed on Christmas Eve all covered up and warm I could almost hear him outside and on top of the house. On Christmas morning I would race downstairs and find beautiful pies, cakes, homemade ice cream and so much to eat and enjoy I couldn't believe my eyes.

My father worked for the Frisco Railway Company making two dollars a day which didn't go very far when he had a wife and seven kids at home depending on him to feed and clothe them. There was on one general store in town and many times my mother would have me walk to the store and get a dozen eggs on credit until my dad got paid. My mother would sew and make a dress for a lady that lived down on the highway for $1.50 and a gallon of milk. One day while walking to the general store I found a nickel on the roadway and couldn't wait until I got back home to tell everyone. Now days when I see an old Western movie it reminds me of our home town because our main street was gravel and dirt just like in the movies. On one side of main street we had wooden sidewalks in front of the buildings.

There was no such thing as a police department, fire department or hospital. The men in town built a metal cage which they placed in an empty room in an empty building. The cage could hold 3 or 4 people and that was called the jailhouse. When someone started acting off the wall, getting drunk and disorderly or doing a criminal act citizens would take him into custody and place him in the metal cage. He would stay there until the Sheriff came to town which was usually on Saturday and take him to the courthouse in the next town for a hearing. I had one uncle on my mother's side that usually stayed drunk on his ass. One day another drunken friend of his turned up shot to death. My uncle was charged with the killing but the authorities couldn't prove it so the judge sentenced him to one year in the county jail anyway. Most people didn't have money to hire a lawyer so they defended themselves. There was no such thing as a public defender working for you.

STORY

My oldest brother built a small wooden building on the highway in front of our house, painted it and called it the Green Oak Club. Between my father and brother they tried to open a store which never amounted to anything. My brother placed a juke box in the place in an effort to attract some kind of business but it was all in vain. We had relatives in Greenwood Springs, Mississippi who had an old pickup truck and they would come to our place on occasion, load the juke box on their truck and haul it back to their place in Mississippi for entertainment on special occasions. During my young lifetime there weren't many days that you could call special. I'll never forget that day I was sitting on our front porch and my dad came upon the porch, gave me a box of Cheese Crackers and a beautiful pair of shoes. I remember what good times we had as well as the bad times. Our lives in that poor little town was nothing but hard times. Sometimes my father would ask me if I was ever going to amount to anything. Living the way we were I can now understand why he ask the question.

I learned early in life that when my father would ask me or told me to do something I should never respond by say, huh? Yes sir and no sir was the only acceptable response and you would only be reminded one time.

Like all the other shit kicking kids in the area I did things that I shouldn't have done because in those days on a broken down farm there wasn't much to do for entertainment. You either did your swimming in the Buddyhatchey River or in the water tank by the railroad tracks for watering train locomotives. We'd sneak around behind our parent's backs and smoke too. We were always broke and buying a pack of cigarettes was out of the question. Most everyone that smoked bought tobacco rolled their own cigarettes. For myself I would rather smoke crossvine that grew in various trees or I'd smoke corn silk and roll my own cigarettes. Anyone born and raised in the country will know exactly what I'm talking about. I never had the money to buy

HARD TIMES

gum so in place of it I'd pull a piece of tar out of a construction barrel and chew it.

The singer Elvis Pressley was born in a one bedroom house in a small town in Mississippi and when I heard him sing the song "Polk Salad Annie" I knew that he must have had the same hard times that I had growing up. Picking and cooking polk salad went a long way in keeping our family from starving. One positive thing about being born and living poor is that you won't realize it. I never knew that I was poor until I heard my first grade teacher say it. Back home in Alabama I don't recall ever seeing over weight or fat people working in the fields. I suppose that if you hoe corn all day long in the field from sun up to sun down it has a way of burning up calories and keeping a person nice and slim. Bending over and picking cotton all day long in the hot Summer sun does wonders for a person's appetite. Working the fields was hard enough for the adults much less a kid in elementary school. Our school house only had one large room divided into six sections for grades first through sixth. All the grades were taught by one and only teacher. During harvest time school was dismissed at noon in order for the students to go home and help their parents work the fields. My mother made me a cotton sack for picking cotton. She would have me follow behind her and pick the cotton pods that she missed.

I always hear kids these days complain about not having a playground or some place for them. Well, the spoiled poor little things don't know how lucky they are that areas are created just for them to play in. When I was a kid I had to play and entertain myself in my back yard which was part of a lumber yard and a side track for storing railroad box cars. We had to entertain ourselves climbing on the huge stacks of lumber and chasing each other around and on top of the box cars, every source of entertainment we had was created by us and we didn't spend our time whining.

Every night as I went to bed on a large thick fluffy mattress under the light of a kerosene lamp I always said a little prayer. "Now I lay me down to sleep, I pray the Lord my soul to keep, if I should die before I wake, I pray the Lord my soul to take." My mother taught me that little prayer when I was just a little boy and I will always say it until the day I die.

On the farm the only way a person could survive and provide for his family was to start making whiskey and being a boot legger. My dad dug a big hole in the pasture and covered it with large timbers and on top of the timbers he placed a large pile of tree limbs and trash. He placed a still in the hole for making whiskey and ran a stove pipe up through the pile of trash. When he was making whiskey the smoke would go out of the stove pipe and make it look like he was burning trash. I guess you could call it a good business adventure because he never got caught. Most people these days don't understand how car racing came about. Some people made their living hauling whiskey and being chased by the police. As a result over time the drivers started racing each other and the sport of car races was born.

I had a Uncle Grover that always bragged about going through the University of Alabama and I bought it until it was revealed that he only went through the University of Alabama selling turnip greens.

As I've stated before in a previous book, my dad went to Miami, Florida looking for work because he realized that none of us was going to amount to anything if we didn't move out of Beaverton and go someplace else. My mother put the farm place up for sale and finally sold it. She sold the entire place which included 80 acres and all the buildings for $1,000 dollars. At that time it was considered big money considering that my father was only making two dollars a day working for the railroad.

HARD TIMES

Everyone has had those heart breaking days. I get so attached to animals that I grieve for weeks when I lose a beloved pet. Recently my heart was broken and it destroyed my zest for life when someone ran over and killed my pet. Being a crippled old man of 84 years dying in my sleep would be a thankful gift. I get so tired of being hurt and disappointed that death doesn't seem that bad anymore. Laying me down underneath the green grass of home and being with my departed family would be a thing to rejoice.

In this life I've acknowledged that we're all born ignorant but some people work hard as hell to become stupid. It is finally recognized that you just can't fix stupid and it seems like most of those become lawyers, politicians and judges. There's a logical reason why some people are more intelligent then others and it doesn't have anything to do with higher education. A person's genes will determine his or her level of intelligence. A study was conducted some years back to prove the point. Place two very young children of different ethnic backgrounds into the same room exposing both to identical environments and observe the difference over time. One child will become more intelligent than the other. The only possible answer is genetics and the acceptance of the theory will place you in the category of being a bigot by the less intelligent. Intelligent people make and create a fortune where ignorant people develop the Robin Hood syndrome. They rob from the rich and have no intention of giving it to the poor. It makes about as much sense as a naked woman sitting on her boy friend's face as she dials 911 complaining that she's being taken advantage of.

It's easy to misunderstand a person when they are telling you something. A friend told me once that he knew for a fact that my neighbor was known for eating a pussy. The thought scared the hell out of me because my wife and I had a beautiful little pussycat and I sure as hell didn't want him to eat it. I ran into our house and told my wife what I was told and to keep our darling little pussycat inside the house. I couldn't believe my wife's attitude and what she said. She said that there was nothing wrong or unusual about our neighbor eating a pussy. I thought that I must be going out of my mind or she has lost hers. I will never understand why anyone would ever want to eat a poor little pussycat.

The one thing that really pisses me off is for women to use abortion as a birth control. In my opinion every woman seeking an abortion should be required to visit a Medical Examiner's Office and look at an unborn baby floating and preserved in a mason jar. Study that perfectly formed little baby and realize that it represents what she's about to kill. Abortion is nothing but another word for murder. We scream about the millions of lives that was snuffed out by Adolph Hitler and Joseph Stalin but don't give any consideration to the 60 million unborn babies murdered since 1973 when it was approved by Roe vs Wade in the United States Supreme Court. Women and people in general think nothing more of murdering an unborn baby then drinking an RC cola and eating a moon pie. Human beings breed like flies and it will never end because most men and women will lie, steal, cheat and even kill for a strange piece of ass.

Unfortunately my first wife fell into that category and I'll never forget those hurtful words spoken to me, "you make my skin crawl." It was just another event among many that destroyed my happiness and family. In retrospect I discovered that I had numerous competitors and my marriage was a lost cause not worth fighting for. The three little words that the wife doesn't want to hear when she's getting laid is "honey I'm home."

Before joining the Dade County Sheriff's Office I worked for Southern Bell Telephone Company for six years . The telephone service back then was $3.55 a month for a four party line, $4.80 for a two party line and $6.00 a month for a private line. Some things I don't think I'll ever forget. I was paid $42.50 a week or $1.05 an hour.

HARD TIMES

The serial number of my first bicycle was B4998 and our home telephone number was 78-1985. It was the first telephone that I ever talked on. My sister's girlfriend Betty Thompkins, lived a block away and I must have driven her crazy calling her number 77-149 all the time just to get to talk to someone on the telephone. Back home in Alabama I never even saw a telephone much less get to talk on one. It seemed like my entire family had to endure undeserved hard times especially during world war two. As I indicated in my book "America, love it or get the hell out" I resent hearing freeloaders sitting on their ass and bitching about everything underneath the sun. Those assholes don't have any idea what hard times are. When I hear Dolly Parton, sing about the coat of many colors that her mother made for her, I know that she must have lived and survived the same way my family lived. My mother didn't make me a coat of many colors but she did make me pretty clothes out of empty flour sacks. Between Dolly Parton and singer Eddie Arnold, it seems like they have identified my life. Dolly identifies my childhood and Arnold identifies my unrelenting broken heart and hopelessness. When he sings "make the world go away and take it off my shoulders because this time Lord you've given me a mountain that I may never be able to climb." In a state of despair I often wake up in the morning disappointed that I'm still alive.

The more I experience life the more I love the animal world and the more I dislike the human race, especially lawyers, politicians and judges are no exception. The biggest assholes that I've ever met in my life were lawyers and judges. Most of those assholes dedicate their lives to screwing people at every turn. Now we have so-called preachers ripping off large companies and it's all quite legal. One hair lip racist has made a fortune threatening to sue companies over discrimination. He will examine the company's records to see how many blacks are employed by the company and if any hold supervisory positions. Then he notifies the company that he intends to file a federal lawsuit against them for discriminating against blacks. The company will always settle the case out of court and pay the racist off to avoid an expensive defense. It's nothing but a blatant case of extortion and the racist community organizer keeps repeating the same scenario over and over.

Then we have the other so-called preacher that's nothing but a sheep herder that spends a whole lot of time going to the White House oval office to talk to the then President Obama. As a matter of fact it has been said that he made 176 trips to the oval office. Like I have previously pointed out I met this loud mouth racist asshole back in the 60's when he was a fat ass, long haired trouble maker with a mustache. At the time I was a deputy sheriff in Miami, Florida and had to kick his fat ass out of the police station for creating a disturbance. That night the jerk made a statement that I have yet to figure out. As he was leaving the station he said "if a humming bird had any brains it would fly backwards." Of course his fans clapped and thought that he was so intelligent. Over the years he has become a skinny little runt with enough grease on his hair to service a fleet of cars.

I suppose your life is determined by which school of hard knocks that you've had to endure. Many times I've had to accept the obvious fact that I might not make it in some endeavor and accepted pending failure. I'll always remember sitting on the floor in front of my dad as I polished his shoes and he would ask me "son, do you think you'll ever amount to anything?" At that time I had no idea what life held for me but over time I realized that it would only be my decision and no one else's to make something out of myself.

At least a funny story had a way of cheering me up when I felt down. Like the story of Little Red Riding Hood walking through the woods to visit her grandmother when suddenly the big bad wolf jumped out in front of her and told her that he was going to eat her. Little Red Riding Hood was really frightened and asked the big bad wolf "if he was going to eat her whole" and the wolf responded, "no I'm going

HARD TIMES

to spit that part out." In my opinion I think he's going to spit the best part out but that's my opinion for what it's worth.

People always question the description of our outhouse back on the farm in Alabama. I'll go through it one more time and not believing is your problem which I can't understand. The outhouse was a two holer which was to accommodate two people at the same time if necessary and yes there was no such thing as soft fluffy rolls of toilet paper. Our toilet paper was pages torn out of a Sears Roebuck catalog which was kept in the outhouse.

Most people just don't understand human behavior and I doubt that they ever will. For example, the male species comes out of a vagina at birth and will spend his entire life trying to get back in. Some will lie, steal, cheat and even commit murder for it. It's important that women fully realize that their vagina can get them killed faster then anything they can buy in a drug store.

Being a devout animal lover I resent hell out of hunters killing any animal and calling it a sport. Some idiot will put out sweet corn to attract a deer then sit in a blind waiting to blow the poor animal's brains out. The way I've been treated by certain elements of society most humans are repugnant to me. Lawyers are on top of the list considering how they make a living. Take the case of Talcum Powder and cervical cancer. Why some woman wanted to sprinkle Talcum Powder on her muff and on the crotch of her panties is beyond my understanding. After years of using Talcum Powder she happened to come down with cervical cancer and all the lawyers couldn't believe such good luck for their profession. The women started hiring lawyers and filing lawsuits against the company making the powder claiming that it caused their cancers. Of all things the court ruled on one woman's behalf and awarded her something like 400 million dollars. Completely ridiculous and for that kind of money I'll snort the shit, sprinkle it on my pecker, put it in my coffee and cereal every morning. I have always been a student of oral sex and now I suspect that someday I may come down with some form of mouth cancer as a result of Talcum Powder. With my luck the court would probably rule that I was some kind of pervert and have me arrested and jailed.

I was just informed that a lot of blacks have stopped buying aspirin because they resent having to pick the cotton out of the bottle. Have you ever heard of anything so silly? In my younger days in the cotton fields in Alabama I picked my share of cotton and there's no comparison picking it out of an aspirin bottle, so don't be so touchy.

Anyone that has lived on the street of hard times will understand why I have the feelings that I do toward certain people. On top of my shit list are lawyers, judges and most politicians. For over 20 years I had a sorry ass lying bitch of a lawyer filing one lawsuit after another against me on behalf of a trailer trash couple that I will refer to as AJ and DJ. The husband is a sexual predator and his douche bag wife is a dangerous psychopath. In the year 1998 the trash produced and distributed hundreds of slanderous posters with my wife's picture all over the county. They posted them in stores, on power poles, in shopping centers, to all our neighbors and even on the front door of our church house for everyone to see on Sunday morning.

I filed a lawsuit against the trash for slander and libel and was awarded a $35,000.00 judgment against them. Prior to going to court I had the Buncombe County Sheriff's Office investigate the incident and the husband AJ admitted to the police that he had a picture of my wife but gave it to his wife prior to the slanderous posters being produced. The officer was unable to contact the wife because she immediately fled to South Florida to avoid any contact with the police. It was learned that the trailer trash couple was a perfect example of freeloaders and had been ripping off the system for years. At present they are ripping off the state of Florida and have had 32 addresses. To hide their way of life they attend a Baptist church in Plantation, Florida professing to be wonderful Christians . They obtained the services of a female lawyer of the Grunt and Dump law firm that we will refer to as Douche Bag Mary. This sorry bitch has no conscience or boundaries on what she will do for money. To avoid my judgment against the trailer trash she filed bankruptcy for them in 2003 and again in 2011 to avoid paying 30 other debts.

Being in law enforcement for 25 years and seeing how lawyers operated I lost all respect for them and the court judges. In my particular case and how I was treated so unfairly, the Rule of Law and Due Process is nothing but a lot of meaningless bullshit. Rest assured lawyers are just well dressed thieves with a license to steal. The assholes will file a lawsuit for the slightest thing. If you have doubts or don't believe so then fart on a crowded elevator in the presence of a lawyer and see how long it takes for you to receive a subpoena to appear in court for violating the clean air act of the Environmental Protection Agency. One time I was on an elevator when a nice looking young lady stepped in and stood in front of me. After a few moments without turning around she ask me if I had a roll of quarters in my pocket or was I just glad to see her?

Well, back to the robbery. As often as Douche Bag Mary was filing lawsuits against me it was common knowledge that she could obtain anything she wanted from a circuit court judge in Fort Lauderdale, Florida. The judge would sign anything she ask for including affidavits even after being told that they were completely based on perjury. It made me wonder what Douche Bag was paying him with. As unbelievable as it was the lying bitch obtained such a high judgment against me you would think that I was an axe murderer or something. By the ruling it was obvious that the presiding judge had his head up his ass. Before the hearing I had asked the judge for a continuance to give me time to find someone to care for my disabled son and for me to get a loan in order for me to make the trip. The judge denied me a continuance which placed me on notice that the judge was obviously

STORY

on Douche Bag Mary's team. I have appeared in court hundreds of times during my law enforcement career and judges would issue a continuance to defendants for just asking and not even requiring an explanation. Needless to say the hearing was held without me and the judge issued a $151,865.00 judgment against me. Apparently he thought that I was a serial killer or something. Talk about a miscarriage of justice, bear in mind that the lawsuit was based entirely on affidavits that were sworn under perjury which the judge had been informed of.

Being financially broke due to all of the lawsuits filed against me I had to file bankruptcy or lose everything I had.

Being that I had a $35,000.00 judgment against the trailer trash that I never did try to collect, I was never notified that they had filed bankruptcy in 2003 and that the bankruptcy court satisfied the judgment against them. Their dip shit lawyer or anyone else never did notify me or my wife that the judgment had been satisfied by a court. Bear in mind that the trailer trash owed 30 different people and businesses including my judgment. Not knowing that my judgment had been satisfied I renewed the judgment because it was going to expire due to the ten year limitation to keep it active. When I renewed it with a local lawyer he failed to check to make sure it was still active. After he renewed the judgment my lawyer received a telephone call from the trailer trash husband AJ advising him that the judgment had been satisfied by court order in 2003 which none of us knew anything about.

The next thing I know their dip shit lawyer in Fort Lauderdale, Florida, Douche Bag Mary filed another lawsuit against me for "willfully and knowingly violating a court order" which was nothing but a crock of bullshit. On numerous occasions I had asked her why didn't she notify me or my wife that the judgment had been satisfied and her response was "I didn't have to notify you of anything and that's your problem not hers." I sent the circuit court judge in Fort Lauderdale,

HARD TIMES

Florida two letters telling him that the lawyer admitted to me on two occasions that I was never notified of the judgment being satisfied and that wasn't her problem. The circuit court judge couldn't care less about the lawyer lying, me being unable to appear in court or giving me a continuance and issued the $151,865.00 judgment against me. Being that I live in Asheville, North Carolina the lying bitch lawyer hired a law firm in Ashville to collect the judgment.

A court hearing was held in Ashville by a Superior Court judge that reinforced my belief that most judges are assholes and over paid. This particular judge didn't even recognize that I was even in the courtroom or ask me one question during the entire hearing. He had one of the slanderous posters and a written explanation of what had occurred in front of him yet he didn't have one question. I'm totally convinced that he never even looked at or read anything that I had written. Worse than that I don't think he even knew anything about the state law "tenants by the entirety" which I was requesting to be ruled on. He appeared to be nothing more than a potted plant and at times I thought that he had gone to sleep.

The lawyer that was trying to stick it up my ass argued that my wife and I had gotten a divorce sometime in our lives and it prevented us from being protected by the state law "tenants by the entirety" which states that each spouse owns 100% of the property and no one can touch it. The lawyer couldn't produce one document to show that we had ever gotten a divorce. He didn't have one iota of proof and yet the simple minded judge ruled that we were "tenants in common" and signed an order drew up by the lawyer directing the sheriff of the county to auction off all our personal possessions, household furnishings, cars and our house to pay the judgment.

Four years before the summary judgment was issued against me, my wife and I had renewed our wedding vows in the Buncombe County Courthouse and we should never have been denied the protection of the state law. Hopefully the Superior Court judge and the asshole lawyer will die and rot in hell where they belong for destroying my life. What they have done to me will be etched in my mind and soul for the rest of my life. Someday with any luck I'll be able to use their grave sites as my personal latrines. In my 25 years testifying in courts I have never observed a bigger moron then that particular Superior Court judge. Actually his demeanor didn't even come up to the level of a potted plant. I had to borrow $130,000.00 to pay the trailer trash or have everything I own auctioned off according to the court order signed by the half witted judge.

It's still unbelievable that a freeloading trailer trash couple produced and distributed hundreds of slanderous posters with my wife's picture all over the county and I had to end up paying them a small fortune for doing it. If this is what they call justice then I want no part of it.

In my years on this earth I've been educated by dealing with hard times. A woman will marry a man in the false belief that she can change him and a man will marry a woman in the false believe that she will stay the same. Here is a good bit of information for the horny people that need some strange loving. Hang out in a gym because that's where you'll get laid if it's going to happen. Horny people recognize that gyms serve as modern whore houses and it's the ideal way of cheating on your spouse. It's the perfect place to find sexual predators and they always start off being real complimentary to the female and before she knows it they just have a cup of innocent coffee after a workout. Within a short period of time she will find herself without her panties and her self respect, she'll be in love and she'll give him money, flowers, jewelry and herself without even thinking of her husband. Ladies, it doesn't matter if you're ugly as sin, fat and stink like hell, men will jump your bones at the slightest opportunity and either party being married doesn't have a thing to do with it. Almost all men will feed a line of bullshit to a woman and have her panties off before she even knows his full name. He'll tell her that she is so

HARD TIMES

beautiful she should be a movie star and he hopes that her husband appreciates her. He will have an endless stream of bullshit and if she was his wife or girlfriend he would treat her like the queen that she is. It will continue until she finds herself in bed at the local Holiday Inn getting her brains screwed out.

When men get my age they usually don't know if they're cumming or going when they're having sex. Of course dying in the saddle would be a great way of going and at least you would display a happy face in the casket during the funeral.

The hard times of my life began when I was just a young boy back in Beaverton, Alabama. My family was dirt poor and poverty was just an accepted way of life. It seems that I was dealt a losing hand my entire life that I've had to live with. As a young teenager in Miami, Florida I mowed lawns for $1.50 and sold newspapers. When I was in the third grade in Shadowlawn Elementary School I only weighed 54 pounds and looked like a refugee from a concentration camp. They had a lunch program for the poor kids at the school and I was given fifty cents a week to pay the cafeteria in order to eat lunch. An older lady that worked in the cafeteria by the name of Mrs. Parks, always helped my tray in a generous way because I looked so under nourished. They finally had me work in the cafeteria during lunch time so I wouldn't have to pay anything and have plenty to eat. Every Friday I would get paid twenty five cents after I finished doing the dishes and cleaning up. I'll never forget how proud I felt having a real job and making money of my own. On the way home I would stop at Harvey's Market and buy myself an RC cola and a bag of peanuts.

Everyday after school my older brother and I had to do all of the house work at home before we could go out and play. Our mother worked at the Miami Delux Laundry for $12.00 a day and just didn't have time to clean the house before going to walk the 13 blocks to work. My older brother and I would go behind the laundry and pick up enough wire coat hangers that we would use to get into the movie house. We would go to the Strand Theater located near the laundry and they'd let us in to see the movie for six coat hangers apiece. Every Saturday the theater would show a serial and we never wanted to miss it. Over the months I saw various serials like the Iron Claw, The Green Hornet, Spy Smasher, The Shadow and of course numerous Western serials. We had two fairly close by theaters that we could go to and get in for nine cents or six wire coat hangers. The Strand which was located at N.W. 7th Avenue and 31st street and the Center was located at N.W. 7th Avenue and 61st street. When World War 2 ended I was sitting in the Center Theater watching the movie Guardsmen. My older sister Dot, came to the theater to get me because she said that everyone was acting crazy because the war had ended and our mother was afraid that I might get hurt.

During the war we had we had Air Raid Wardens working with Civil Defense that would check the neighborhoods to made sure that everyone had turned off all their house lights whenever we had an air raid drill.

My two oldest brothers had joined the United States Navy when Pearl Harbor was bombed. The Department of the Navy let them serve on the same ship until all five Sullivan brothers got killed being on the same ship. When that happened the Naval Department prohibited having family members serving on the same ship and separated my brothers. One was assigned to the USS Dupont and the other brother was assigned to the USS Edison, both destroyers.

As I've stated before I was born dirt poor and lived most of my life in a state of poverty. It never ends and everything is in a state of change. Even old accepted sayings like "The love of money is the root of all evil" has changed over time with out question. The present day of truth is "The love of sex is the root of all evil." Look about you and behold all of the evilness that happens to totally innocent people for some persons sexual gratification. In my opinion it's paramount that young females should be educated regarding the perils of sex at an early age. They should be made to understand that there are sick men that will go to any length to violate them sexually even if it requires taking their life. In my opinion the conviction of rape should carry the death penalty in every state.

The one thing that should be abolished immediately is Parole Boards. If an individual is sentenced to ten years he should serve every day of ten years. Giving prisoners time off their sentence for not causing problems is nothing but bullshit and certainly doesn't discourage potential criminals from violating the law. There are do gooders that think if you give a prisoner time off his sentence for not causing trouble it will encourage him to be a Mr. Goodie Two Shoes and be a model prisoner. My position is rather simple. If a prisoner causes trouble and problems you simply add more time to his sentence.

Regarding Parole Boards in my opinion they are nothing but a magnet for bribes. It's a fast and easy way of getting someone out of jail. There are people that won't hesitate for a second to pay a member of the Parole Board to grant parole to a particular prisoner. When a person is sentenced to a long period of time in jail they become institutionalized and you can't drag them out of jail. It becomes a way of life and they have no desire of rejoining the general population on the outside. In prison they get three square meals a day with plenty of deserts, a basketball court, movies and law library to just name a few. Where else could they live such a good life free of charge?

It's common knowledge that drugs find their way into prison and are made available to the inmates for their enjoyment. The United States Supreme Court has ruled that it's cruel and unusual punishment to deprive a prisoner female ass, so now the ladies are permitted to go into prisons and screw the prisoners to heavenly bliss. Sometimes I feel that I'd be better off in jail then outside working my ass off to survive and at least I know that I could get laid by the ladies.

Sometimes I don't think I'll ever be able to get off the boulevard of hard times and it's just one mountain after another to climb. I've always tried to be a good person and treat other people like I wanted to be treated. Trying to live by the Golden Rule didn't seem to work out for me and as I grew older my health went to hell in a hand basket. After two strokes , a couple heart attacks and back surgery it left me a shell of the man I use to be. Now I'm just a crippled old man that survives from one day to the next. I guess that I should consider myself lucky that I'm still alive even though I have one foot in the grave and the other foot on a banana peel. Even at my rotten old age I still enjoy humor and a good joke. For example, a young man's first train trip comes to mind. He was assigned the lower sleeper on a long trip and one night he was woke up by the couple on the sleeper above him. He asked them what the hell they were doing to disturb his sleep? After a slight hesitation they said that they were making a sandwich. The young man told them to be more careful with the mayonnaise because some had fallen down on his face. Between that young man and the other young man working at the local grocery store as a bag boy sometimes life can be a mystery. As he was helping a nice looking older lady with her shopping cart through the parking lot, the lady told him that she had an itchy pussy and the young man responded telling her that she would have to point the car out because all the Japanese cars looked alike to him.

Sometimes I think that the interesting little stories is the one thing that keeps me from falling apart and just giving up on life. I've been kicked around and mistreated enough to resent most people. It has gotten to the point that I don't trust anyone and live by the Mafia creed of keeping your friends close but your enemies closer. I don't believe anything I read and only half of what I hear. Never tell a friend of everything you know because then he will become a whole lot smarter than you because they will know your business plus theirs. Always remember that there are two sides to every story so take what you hear with a grain of salt. Your friend today may well be your biggest enemy tomorrow. Speak softly but always carry a big stick and above all never corner a coward because his fear will get you killed.

In my 25 years in law enforcement I learned early how undivided attention can get you killed when you're in a confrontational situation. Today a marine or any service person would be safer stationed in Iraq or Afghanistan than Chicago or some other big city in America. We have over 30 million illegal immigrants in our country today and they keep pouring in by the hundreds of thousands looking for the good life. I've said it before and I'll keep saying it until hell freezes over, big business looking for cheap labor caused the entire immigration problem. Half of the people I see coming into our country are knocked up females from Mexico and other Central American countries. They get knocked up down there and then run for the American border to squirt out the baby because they know being born in America will make it a citizen of America which is a lot of bullshit as far as I'm concerned. In my home town of Asheville, North Carolina we're beginning to have wall to wall Mexican looking people. Most seem to drive new pickup trucks and work mainly for construction companies. With the help of the Socialist Democratic Party the white Anglo-Saxon people will no doubt become extinct in the future.

People today bitch and object to everything and displays a level of ignorance that's unbelievable. In Asheville they're known as CAVE people. Citizens that Are Virtually against Everything. Again it's like actor John Wayne said, "Life is tough and it's a lot tougher when you're stupid." Even in my home town we have ugly looking fat women covered with tattoos sitting in front of the police station exposing their sagging tits to everyone. Walking around with their ugly flopping tits exposed doesn't seem to violate any law according to the

STORY

police. If the Mayor and city commission doesn't wake up the city will become a cess pool of low life trash.

I have discovered that a person doesn't need a doctor to tell him that he's dying because Mother Nature will tell him and she will do it for free. When a person enters the twilight years of his or her life the mysteries of life will become evident. An old person will become smart when it's too late to change things. There are things to question and there are things that should be left alone. I am convinced that a person's path of life is determined the day you are borned.

The words of Plato has always stuck in my mind and rings so true today. "All forms of government destroys themselves by carrying their basic principle to excess, the democracies become too free, in politics and economics, in morals, even in literature and art until at last even the puppy dogs in our house rise up on their hind legs and demand their rights...disorder grows to such a point that society will abandon all it's liberty to anyone who can restore order."

Apparently Plato knew what he was talking about because our country is presently faced with such a crisis.

There has been some hard times in my life but the one that really stands out was when the trashy ass lying female lawyer known as Douche Bag Mary in Plantation, Florida started filing lawsuits against me in 1998. If you're interested in finding out how the Legal System, Rule of Law and Due Process can destroy your life read the book "Kangaroo Justice and Well Dressed Thieves With a License to Steal" and you'll know how easily it's done. When I get depressed thinking about how I got robbed by the sorry ass lawyers and judges I always remind myself of a humorous joke. When I was a younger drinking man I went to my favorite neighborhood bar for a cool beer after work and was busy minding my own business when a nice looking lady walked into the bar and sat down on the stool next to me. When

HARD TIMES

the bartender served me my drink he had pushed a bowl of nuts in front of me to have with my beer. Being the gentleman that I am I pushed the bowl of nuts over to her and asked her if she'd like to eat my nuts and that's how the fight got started. She completely misunderstood my intention and promptly knocked me off the bar stool. People should be more careful and not jump to conclusions when asked a simple question.

It reminds me of the time three men were sitting in the waiting room at the doctor's office. All three men had basically the same problem. One gentleman had red balls, one gentleman had green balls and the third gentleman had brown balls. The receptionist called the man with the red balls in to see the doctor. When he came out of the examination room the receptionist charged him $25.00. Then she told the man with the green balls to go into the examination room for the doctor. When he came out the receptionist charged him $250.00 which really upset the gentleman . He ask her why the hell was she charging him so much when she only charged the prior patient $25.00? She very politely told him that there was a big difference between lipstick and gangrene. Later that evening the gentleman with the brown balls got home after work and really got upset over the condition of the house and complained to his wife. The beds weren't made up, the kitchen sink was full of dirty dishes and dirty clothes were scattered all over the living room floor. While complaining to his wife and asking her what the hell had she been doing all day, she responded that she had been so busy all day with the kids she didn't have time to wipe her ass to which he replied "yes and that's something else I want to talk to you about."

Every young person growing up will always remember their very first love and I'm no exception. When I was in high school at Miami Edison I fell madly and hopelessly in love with a beautiful majorette at Miami Jackson High School. Her father was a type setter at the Miami Herald newspaper and after going on a labor strike he took his family and moved to Galveston, Texas to get a job. Every day during my fifth period class of effective living taught by Mr. Hudson, I always wrote a letter to my majorette. Her name was Gail Ackerman and she was the most beautiful girl that I had ever seen in my entire young life. Every day I would mail her a letter addressed to 1218 South Bayou Shore Drive in Galveston, Texas. When she wrote to me she would always write S.W.A.K. on the back of the envelope which meant "sealed with a kiss" and if you love me you'll always remember this.

When school let out for the Summer I drove my 1941 Ford coupe to Galveston, Texas to see her. We made plans to go to the movie and when I picked her up at her house she was an absolute angel of my dreams and as beautiful as ever. We went to see the movie Prisoner of Zenda with James Mason and after the movie we parked on the high sea wall and talked about old times while in Miami. She looked so beautiful in her white blouse and sparkling hazel eyes. When I returned to Miami I still loved everything about her and lived on the beautiful memories of her. I carried her picture in my billfold for 60 years never seeing her again. She was never absent from my mind and memory. Many nights I would dream about Gail and weep in my sleep being without her. For years I searched the internet for her to no avail. Numerous times I thought that I had found her but the person never responded to me and I never knew for sure if it was her. It would have done me a world of good and my prayers answered if only I could have talked to her one more time but it was not to be.

Sometimes life can seem to be so cruel to an innocent heart and especially to a young person who experiences his or her first love. Unless you have lived such an experience you'll never understand how I felt and my hurt feelings. What is a tragedy to a young person isn't usually understood by grown ups and including parents. Sometimes it seem like I was confronted with one mountain after another and I simply didn't know what to do with myself. I was so busy trying to find myself I didn't take the time to appreciate all of the good and

HARD TIMES

positive things in my life. It never occurred to me that the best things in life were free because in my mind I was always struggling to be something else.

I was born dirt poor and in my mind there just didn't seem to be a way out. For years before moving to Miami my family never enjoyed the so-called good life and existed in poverty on a broken down farm in Alabama. While living in Alabama a lumber yard and railroad tracks were located at the rear of our house and that was my play ground as a young kid. My parents realized that the family was never going to amount to anything as long as we were going to live in the pathetic little town. Life was a struggle to survive and there wasn't any such thing as food stamps and welfare programs to help down and out people.

I never knew what it was to ride in a car and eat an ice cream cone until I was a teenager living in Miami, Florida. Walking to school and every other place that I wanted to go was the only way to get around when I was a teenager in Alabama and Florida. During one Christmas in Florida my mother bought a used bicycle for my older brother and I to ride to school. After school each day when I was in the tenth grade I would stand on the corner and watch a student by the name of Jackie Walker leave and drive his new Ford pass the front of the school house. I didn't have a car to drive around the school house waving to everyone but at least I had a bicycle and didn't have to walk anymore. It became a goal of mine to own a car someday so I started mowing lawns, selling news papers and any other odd jobs I could find to make some money. I got a news paper route with the Miami Herald and put $2.00 a week in a bond that I carried with the company until I finally saved up enough to buy myself a broken down 1941 Ford. It wasn't much to look at and my brother in law taught me how to drive it. Maybe I was driving a pile of junk but it made me feel like I was the King of the road. I didn't have a bicycle that I could call my own but now I actually had a car that was all mine. Selling newspapers didn't pay very much so when I needed a tire I would buy a used one or a recap and gasoline was only 22 cents a gallon.

At school my car never impressed anyone including a pretty little blond that I had eyes for by the name of Iris Maxwell. Iris never even knew that I existed and neither did a close neighbor of mine by the name of Shirley Wells. She was an outrageously beautiful little red head that walked by my house everyday after school. I was at that awkward age where I couldn't understand the strong physical feelings that had come over me.

We all have disappoints in life and it seems like mine started early. In high school the physical education coach asked me to go out for the varsity football team. When I went home and asked my dad to sign the paper giving me permission to play he refused and told me that I didn't have to break my leg on a football field because he'd do it for me. When a friend of mine, Charles "Spot" Martin, and I took an examination for entry into the United States Air Force Academy we both qualified to attend the academy in Colorado. I was excited beyond words just to think that I was going to be a fighter pilot but my dad raised so much holy hell to my mother over it I withdrew my application. My friend Spot went on to the academy and sent me a picture of him standing on the wing next to the cockpit which had his name inscribed on it, Lieutenant Charles "Spot" Martin. When Spot came home on leave he took me for an airplane ride over Miami and Key Biscayne which I will never forget.

Our military personnel, police officers, fire fighters and other professional people have my utmost respect but what the hell has happened to our youth? The freeloading attitude of too many citizens is why I named a previous book "America, Love It or Get The Hell Out and From The Greatest Generation To The Gutter Generation."

HARD TIMES

It appears that the patriotic feeling of too many citizens has vanished. So called patriotic citizens are bound and determined to drive the American Automobile Industry out of business. When you're on the road look around and you'll notice that 8 out of 10 vehicles on the road are foreign made. Of course some of the proud patriots will stick a decal of an American flag on he bumper of their Toyota. The Japanese may have lost some battles but they won the war. Like I said on the cover of the book, Dirt Poor And Abortion Is Just Another Word For Murder. What little I ever accumulated didn't come easy or was given to me by the government or anyone else. When I see people and especially young people sitting on their ass smoking a joint and bitching I could kick their ass above their shoulders. Most readers don't like to hear the truth because a twisted lie is so much easier to accept and believe. I'm a rogue writer and don't follow the rules and writing rules suck as far as I'm concerned. If I know that a person is an asshole I'll call him one and if he or she doesn't like it then they can kiss my Royal Canadian ass.

Just look at the Socialist Party or better known as the Democratic Party and listen to the flaming asshole that leads the party. That jerk has let the liberal left control the Democratic Party and she may as well just sit down and shut up. I think a face lift and a good swift kick in the ass would do her a lot of good. Too many cigarettes, booze and sun shine will destroy a person's skin and wrinkle them up. All the dip shits in Congress want to fly all over the place at taxpayer's expense and you'll find them lying on the beach at some foreign resort soaking up the sun and getting an ugly complexion. The reason that Congress is so screwed up is there's no term limits and almost all of them are lawyers. I'm sure everyone has heard of born killers and I guess the best way to describe lawyers is born thieves. Everyone should know by now that the driving force to become a lawyer is that you can make a fortune doing nothing but sitting on your ass. Why work when you can occupy a public office and be paid for doing nothing.

Senators and Representatives wear sitting on their lazy worthless ass as a badge of honor. Some of the people serving in Congress are so old they just sit there and drool all over themselves in a stupor. We had one Supreme Court Justice that was so old and out of it they had to push him to attend hearings in a wheel chair as he drooled all over himself. The way Congress is so screwed up I suspect that some are senile and have no idea what the hell is going on. Some of the obvious young morons being elected to Congress now don't know their ass from a hole in the ground. It's hard to believe that such stupid people can actually be elected which shows you how ignorant voters can be.

To make things worse lawyers become judges and that's how we wind up with the country's biggest assholes in the 9th circuit. The biggest assholes I've ever met in my entire life were lawyers and judges that I appeared before in court. I appeared before two of them recently as I was being robbed by a couple lawyers. One was a Superior Court judge in North Carolina and the other one was a Circuit Court judge in Fort Lauderdale, Florida. By their rulings I'm convinced that both are moron level court officers. It's obvious the judge in North Carolina doesn't know or understand the state law regarding "tenants by the entirety" and needs to read up on it before he screws someone else. The Circuit Court judge in Fort Lauderdale, Florida needs to concentrate more on the so called Rule of Law then getting a strange piece of ass.

It's said that we're a nation of laws which makes it fertile ground for lawyers to rip people off. Take it from me, if you fart on a crowded elevator and there's a lawyer on board expect to be sued. You can probably expect a subpoena to appear in court for violating some law with - the Environmental Protection Agency. Cut the cheese standing next to a lawyer and you'll get first hand knowledge on why they say we're a nation of laws.

HARD TIMES

Why anyone would want work so much to become a lawyer and join the band of thieves is beyond me. You don't have to go to the trouble of calling a lawyer just stand on the corner and fart, they'll find you. If you want to find out how sorry lawyers and judges can be read the book "Kangaroo Justice And Well Dressed Thieves With A License To Steal." No one is insulated from a lawyer's wrath. When they smell money they become frenzy sharks in bloody water. The best and sure way of escaping poverty and the struggle to survive is to become a lawyer. If stealing and lying doesn't bother your conscience then you're a perfect candidate for law school. I worked for $1.05 an hour or $42.50 cents a week with Southern Bell Telephone when I graduated out of high school while lawyers were sitting on their ass making more money in one hour then I was in a week of manual labor in the hot sun. Lawyers put John Dillinger and Jesse James to shame when it comes to robbery and they don't even have to wear a mask or have a gun. At present lawyers make $300.00 an hour or $2,400.00 for an eight hour day. I have just been advised by one client that their fee has gone up to $400.00 an hour. That particular client said that his lawyer charges him $200.00 just to read an email from him. At least the lawyer can read which is a plus for his ability. Does all of this information make you feel better for the sorry bastards for having such a hard life? I can only imagine what a dipstick judge makes from the taxpayers.

The country would be a damn site better off if being a lawyer would disqualify a person from holding public office. The best thing going for President Trump is the fact that he's not a lawyer. He thinks and acts like the common working man instead of an idiot like most lawyers. Maybe reenacting dueling might improve things with the operation of the federal government because it appears that it's the only way to get some of them out of office. At least it would get rid of a lot of useless brain dead people out of congress. That way the useless bastards could stop all of their bullshit arguing and shoot ach other.

STORY

In everyones life there's always that one person that becomes special to you. As a teenager I had friends but none could compare with my Syrian friend Bill Barimo, who lived down the street from me. I got to know his family and fell in love with his entire family. His parents always welcomed me at their home and treated me like family including his brother and sisters. Over time I found myself being strongly attracted to my new friend Bill and there was nothing that I wouldn't do for and with him. We're both in our eighties now and I still love him as much as ever. If anyone deserves a good life it's him and I have been truly blessed to have known him and his beautiful family. Sometimes I wonder what I ever did in my life to please the Lord so much that he would give me Bill's friendship for my entire life.

My family consisted of nine, my parents and seven children. A long time ago when a lot of people lived on a farm and raising crops to survive they were inclined to have a lot of children to help with the crops because of the inability to hire help. As a young boy I knew what it was to get up at 4 o'clock in the morning to follow my mother to a cotton field because no one was left home to watch over me. None of my older brothers and sisters could be left behind with me because everyone was needed to work the fields.

After our family moved to Florida my older brother and I would go back to Alabama during the Summertime and help our Uncle Tidy and Aunt Ludie to bring in their crops. Many days I stood at the corner of a ten acre field of corn with a hoe in my hand trying to see the end of a row of corn stalks that I had to hoe.

When I got to the end I would move over to the next row and start back to the other end where I started. Doing the entire field seemed hopeless and it would take days to finish. It really seems ironic because today you almost have to kiss a teenager's ass to get him to mow the lawn much less seeing him stand at the end of a ten acre corn field with a hoe in his hand.

HARD TIMES

Have you ever known somebody that thrives and lives on hate? I had such a woman that my nephew married at a very young age. That sorry ass woman is still alive today and goes by the name of Iris. From the day she married my nephew she expressed an undying hatred for his mother which was my older sister. My nephew couldn't even visit his mother without his wife bitching and raising holy hell. They visited my wife and I in North Carolina and while sitting at the table she said that she despised the ground that my sister walked on. With that statement I had to get up and excuse myself because I suddenly got a very strong urge to reach across the table and slap the shit out of the hateful bitch. How stupid does a person have to be to say something like that to a person about his sister? Her hate was so intense and profound that she never missed an opportunity to express her hate to other people. She would always go out of her way to show her ass and let everyone know how much she hated my sister because it gave her a feeling of joy and satisfaction. When my nephew's father died it didn't matter to Iris that her husband's father had died because she didn't like him either.

The entire family went to my sister's home to offer our respects and support in such a sad and heart breaking time. During the entire time Iris stood outside in front of the house next to the parked cars and refused to come into the house. I finally went outside and asked her why didn't she come into the house with the rest of us and she said that there wasn't anyone in the house that she would like to see. No doubt she was referring to my sister and she was letting everyone present to see how much she hated her. Like I said before her constant goal in life was to show everyone how much she hated her husband's mother.

When all of us went to the church for the funeral services the sorry hateful bitch even went there too so she could stand in front of the church and refuse to come inside. She spent the entire time during the services walking back and forth outside in front of the large glass sliding doors next to where everyone was seated in the church so everyone could see her. I've seen a lot of hateful sorry ass people in my life but that bitch takes first place hands down.

Shortly there after my sister passed away which no doubt was the happiest day of the bitche's life. At last she was finally rid of her husband's mother who was a devout Christian and never said or did anything to hurt another person. No one could ever understand why Iris was so hateful and it was agreed that she had to be mentally ill and in need of mental therapy in a bad way or psychotic drugs to help her. Her behavior was that of a psychopath and she should have been under a doctor's care or in a mental institution.

Here's something that's completely mind boggling to say the least. The day after my sister died my nephew apparently got into a heated discussion with his bitch wife on why she was going to his mother's funeral since she hated her so much. It was common knowledge that the only reason she wanted to go was so she could show everyone how much she hated his mother just like she did with his father. My nephew had a bad case of congestive heart failure and his wife knew it but that didn't keep her from getting him completely upset which caused him to drop over dead from arguing with him. It's common knowledge and his bitch wife knew it that if you get a person with congestive heart failure overly excited and upset it can kill them. Iris knew it but she couldn't shut her hateful damn mouth and continued bitching about his dead mother until he fell over dead on I know that she caused my nephew's death as if I was there listening to the bitch shooting her hateful mouth off to him. Thank God my dear sister didn't have to see her beloved son die. As far as I know the hateful bitch is still alive and hopefully she'll get her rewards when she dies and burns in hell. Someday her children will wake up and realize that she killed their father.

Hard times and disappointments seem to always follow me around when I needed help the most. When I joined the United States Naval

HARD TIMES

Reserve I was proud to serve my country but sometimes I got the opinion that my country wasn't so proud of me. After serving eight years and receiving an Honorable Discharge I went to the Veterans Administration's hospital to get some medicine and was promptly informed that I wasn't eligible to receive anything including medicine. Attending various schools, serving time on two naval destroyer escorts the USS Tills and McCleland didn't mean anything to them. Attending naval boot camp in Providence, Rhode Island and serving time in the Construction Battalion known as the Sea Bees and pouring concrete in the islands for officer's quarters didn't mean anything to them either. Looking back I now realize that I should have joined the army for six months dishing beans so I would be qualified for all the benefits offered to veterans. It was disheartening for me to know that participating in war games at sea involving aircraft, submarines, surface exercises and gunnery practice as a second loader on a twin forties gun mount wasn't considered either. Chipping paint on dept charge racks on a destroyer and attending regular scheduled meetings including drilling on a grinder was as worthless as everything else when asking for help. I never received one simple benefit from the Veteran's Administration but I'm still proud of my Honorable Discharge from the United States Navy hanging on my office wall.

Sometimes it's hard not to feel sorry for yourself especially as you grow old. Generally speaking people just don't want to be bothered by old people. Parents will take care of their children and protect them from harm but it doesn't seem to work the other way around. Old people are usually left alone and have to endure loneliness each and every day. When you know that the last days of your life are numbered it's fed by depression and as I've said before you don't need a doctor to tell you that you're dying because Mother Nature will tell you and do it for free. As you grow older your life long friends start dropping like flies. It has gotten to the point that I don't have any friends left to visit. My last friend Robert Stephenson, dropped over dead without saying a word or making a sound when we were having a cup of coffee together. Between his death and finding my mother dead on her living room floor I realized how fragile life was and started wondering how and when I would suddenly leave my place on this earth.

I'm convinced that the Lord doesn't control all of the events that occur on earth. He gave people "Free Will" and what happens to people is determined by themselves and simply put is an "Accident of Existence." It's certainly not the making of the Lord for people committing suicides, genocides or a bus running off a cliff killing innocent little children. Since 1973 sixty million unborn and tiny little babies have been murdered by so called abortion.

"Blessed are the peace makers for they shall inherit the earth." Love your neighbor like you love yourself and always try and live by the "Golden Rule." Above all, don't present yourself as a Christian when you're not one. The trailer trash couple that tried to destroy my life are big church goers in Plantation, Florida. They sing praises to the Lord every Sunday morning and spends the rest of the week plotting on how to harm someone else. This trashy couple gave new meaning to the word hypocrite. They are honest to goodness real rip off artist and have been ripping off the state of Florida and the federal government for years. Both are worthless bums of the highest degree and have perfected the skills for ripping off the system. Stealing from other people and lying through their teeth about it means nothing to them. The husband is a sexual predator who spends most of his time chasing women and being followed by his insanely jealous psychopathic wife trying to catch him with another woman. He was recently caught with a married woman in Fort Lauderdale and got his sorry ass kicked good from which he claims that he suffered a brain injury. Of all things he applied for a disability from the government and got it. Now he receives a disability on top of what he and his wife can steal. They will run up debts with 30 or 40 businesses and people and then file bankruptcy. As soon as they get rid of those debts they start all over again and usually file another bankruptcy every eight years.

HARD TIMES

I know that the Lord doesn't have anything to do with it but I hope the hell I can out live the trash because it would do me a lot of good and pleasure if I could take a nice dump on their grave sites. Their grave sites would make perfect and well deserved latrines. Their saving salvation is the fact that I'm a cripple and unable to drive otherwise they would have to stand good for what they have done to my life. The trash couple won't work because they're making more than enough money from welfare then they possibly could working. Something is wrong with the system when the bums get paid $125,000.00 and never misses one welfare check from Florida. Between fraud and drug sells why the hell would they ever want to actually go to work? Things couldn't be better for them and they are living high on the hog so to speak.

Those welfare cheats and bums drive nice new cars and I'm lucky to have a 23 year old truck with 300,000 miles on it. Most of the time it's in the garage getting repaired because otherwise my wife and I would have to walk. The mechanic told me that the truck really isn't worth fixing but it has to be repaired because it's impossible for me to buy another vehicle. I had to borrow $125,000.00 on our house to pay the trailer trash for a summary judgment they filed against me which was based on an affidavit that was filed under perjury.

Presently my house payments are $3,500.00 a month as a result of the money that I had to borrow. As I've mentioned before the trailer trash hired a lying bitch lawyer in Plantation, Florida to file a summary judgment against me based completely on a perjured affidavit. The affidavit stated that I "willfully and knowingly violated a court order" which was a damn lie admitted to me on two occasions by their lawyer. Before any court hearing was held I wrote the circuit court judge in Fort Lauderdale, Florida and informed him that the sworn affidavit filed against me was based completely on perjury which the lawyer admitted to me on two separate occasions. That information didn't mean anything to the judge and he apparently placed more value on his relationship with the female lawyer than truth and justice. Judges are human and have the same desires of flesh as other men. Most men have to pay for a piece of ass but apparently a judge can get some for his signature.

Some readers may be surprised and offended by the way I write but you can depend on one thing it will be the truth because make believe is nothing but a waste of paper and time. When I was on the motorcycle squad with the Dade County Sheriff's Office I issued a traffic citation to Cassius Clay who happened to be the heavy weight boxing champion of the world. He gave the ticket to his manager Chris Dundee to take care of which Dundee failed to do. I checked with the court clerk's office and discovered that the ticket had never been paid and the court had issued a bench warrant for Clay's arrest. A few days later I observed Mr. Dundee taking Clay to the gym on Miami Beach for a workout and I stopped them. I informed Mr. Clay that a bench warrant had been issued for his arrest for not paying the ticket and had them follow me to the county jail where Mr. Clay had to post bond. He was a complete gentleman and I felt bad having to arrest him but my job required it. When he appeared in court the judge sentenced him to ten days in jail which I thought was too severe but there was nothing I could do about it. As a matter of fact I still have the traffic ticket that I issued to him in 1966 hanging on my office wall.

Every time I turn on the television set I always see an advertisement for the problem of constipation but I've discovered that I don't need any of their store remedies. All I have to do is turn on the television, look at Joy Behar, Nancy Pelosi or Chuck Shumer and it works better then exlax or anything I can buy in the drug store. For some reason just looking at anyone of them gives me the urge to have a bowel movement. Now when I have to go to the restroom I just tell my wife that I'm going to take a Pelosi or Behar and she knows exactly why I'm going to the restroom.

HARD TIMES

I always stop off at my neighborhood bar for a cool beer on the way home each day. As usual bragging Bob seems to always be there telling everyone that he still has the best nose for smelling then anyone in the country. After weeks of his constant bragging the bar tender finally challenged him to prove it. At that the bar tender went outside and picked up various chips of wood and put them into a box. He went back inside and placed a blindfold over bragging Bob's eyes. Then he held a wood chip underneath Bob's nose and he stated that's birch. Another wood chip was held underneath his nose and he stated that's pine. A third wood chip was held underneath his nose and he stated that's easy it's oak. By this time the bar tender was becoming concerned because each one of them had put up a twenty dollar bet. The bar tender could see that he was going to lose the bet so he told the beautiful bar maid to get on top of the bar counter and stick her ass near his nose. Bob hesitated for a few seconds and then asked the bar tender to turn it over for him. At that the bar maid turned over and stuck her pussy next to his nose. After a few seconds bragging Bob announced you can't fool me, the wood chip is off the shit house door of a tuna boat. Without any objections from anyone Bob picked up the money bet and walked out of the bar.

As a police officer I've had my ass kicked on numerous occasions and getting sucker punched was nothing unusual. The only way I could understand or communicate with a person I was dealing with was to talk to them on their level. Most punks will misinterpret your kindness and politeness as a weakness and will react like a disrespectful punk. Sometimes it results in you having to kick his sorry disrespectful ass to get his attention. A foot in someone's ass always encouraged a better understanding.

I have always supported every law enforcement agency but it took an asshole supervisor to be in charge of raiding consultant Robert Stone's home recently. Special Counselor Mueller, in his zeal to pin something on President Trump, directed the F.B.I. to raid Mr. Stone's home at 6 a.m. with a field force of 29 F.B.I. Agents. Eleven police cars responded with flashing lights with the agents wearing bullet proof vests, night goggles and approached Mr. Stone's house carrying firearms including a AR-15 assault rifle. Then they started pounding on the front door loudly yelling F.B.I. open the door. For the record Mr. Stone did not have a criminal record of any kind or even a jay walking ticket and did not even own a gun. At the time of the show boat raid Mr. Stone was home alone with his wife, three cats and two dogs. During the entire spectacle there was a crowd from the liberal CNN network there filming the entire incident. It was an obvious show put on to intimidate Mr. Stone. Anytime an indictment is issued for anyone in government the standard procedure is to contact the person's attorney and have him turn himself in. In my humble opinion I think that the operation made everyone except Mr. Stone look like a bunch of assholes that deserve no respect. The investigation has cost the taxpayers thirty million dollars and didn't accomplish anything worth while and was just a big waste of time and money. It appears that half of the investigators on the operation were devout Trump haters and if they could have found something on Trump they would have. It was nothing but a witch hunt and everyone knew it.

I see where Governor Cuomo of New York has signed a bill giving women the absolute right to murder their unborn children. Those assholes call it abortion so it doesn't sound so bad but it's still murder. I've said it before and I'll keep saying it until hell freezes over. Before any woman chooses to murder their unborn baby, she should be required to go to a Medical Examiner's Office and view the unborn babies preserved and floating in mason jars.

The people that Adolph Hitler and Joseph Stalin murdered isn't a drop in the bucket that so called abortions have murdered. Hard times has been my life but at least I have a life denied to millions. Thank God I had a loving and caring mother who cherished life and looked upon me as a God's blessing. There weren't many days that my family was

HARD TIMES

free from want but like mom would always say, "we have each other." Sometimes my mind slips back into the past and reminds me of what we didn't have and never missed.

During World War 2 we didn't have the luxuries that most families enjoyed including a high selection of food to eat. I spent a lot of time climbing various fruit trees in the neighborhoods gathering fruit to take home for the family. There was no such thing as food stamps and welfare programs. Apparently some of the neighbors could see how poor we were because one morning mother opened the front door and there sat a big basket of food. In those days people would help each other in any way that they could. That certainly doesn't seem to be the case today considering how my neighbors have treated my wife and I. I'm surrounded by neighbors that spend most of their time trying to mind someone else's business and being hateful about everything. One neighbor across from us is a lying nasty bitch that would rather tell a lie then the truth. She is nothing but a trouble maker that thinks she's the meanest bitch in the valley. Actually she has the fattest ass in the valley but we won't go into that. The neighbor on one side of us is a nice guy that I like but he just doesn't have any balls when it comes to being the head of his house. The neighbor on the other side of is one of those people that never gets over anything. Totally hard headed and a mental case. Everything has to be his way and the question of him ever being wrong is totally ridiculous to even consider. He will go out of his way and do anything he can do to annoy and harass someone.

When I was a young kid just moving to Miami, Florida my parents never had enough money to buy a television set but it didn't really matter that much because there was only one television station in town. I would walk down to Zink's drug store on the corner of North West 7th Avenue and 46 Street to watch television in his store. The owner would have chairs in front of his television set for customers to sit on while watching television. I'll never forget the man Ralph

Renick who broadcast the news and he would always say in closing, "may the good news be your news."

Without a television set I would always sit on the floor in front of our radio and listen to Terry and The Pirates, the Shadow, who would always say "What evil lurks in the hearts of men, the Shadow knows." One of my favorite programs was Hop Harrigan who would open his program by saying "CX4 to control tower this is Hop Harrigan coming in." One day to my mother's surprise a man walked up to the front door and introduced himself as TV Joe and told my mother that he would leave a television set for us to watch for a week free of charge and if she decided that she didn't want it he would pick it up. Needless to say once all of us started watching the television , she kept it. For me there was no more walking to Zink's drug store to watch television.

There's two things that I love on this earth, small children and animals. Almost everything else sucks. Look at the sea of people that are constantly trying to get into the United States. At present our country has thirty million illegal immigrants in our country and they're still pouring in by the thousands. All of the able bodied men immigrants are nothing but a breed of chicken shits too scared to straighten up their own country. This may come as news to ail the nit wits in America but you deserve what you're getting and more. It was just discovered that 58,000 non citizens in Texas voted in the last presidential election. If 58,000 voted in Texas then you can imagine how many voted in all of the other states. Liberal Democrats are fighting any efforts made that requires someone to be a citizen to vote.

I have to show identification to issue a check at the grocery store but no such requirement is made in most states to vote.

America is run mostly by dipstick lawyers and that should tell you why the country is so screwed up. Being a Congressman is a part time job yet they receive full pay for just sitting on their ass doing nothing half the time. Like I've said before being a lawyer should disqualify a person from holding public office. Historically most lawyers have been money thieves and have no conscience of their wrong doings. Like I've said before the best thing going for President Trump is the fact that he's not a lawyer. He's certainly a better and stronger man than 1 am because I couldn't endure the abuse that he has taken. By now I would have been stomping the living shit out of a bunch of news people and morons on talk shows.

Roe vs Wade regarding abortion was the worse decision ever made by the Supreme Court and hopefully it will be reversed in order to save the lives of unborn children. In my opinion the one person that should have been aborted was Governor Cuomo of New York. You will always have some idiot running around saying that no one has the right to tell a woman what she can and cannot do with her body. Women should not have the right to murder another human being and they can scream until hell freezes over and my opinion will never change. If a woman can legally kill someone then I must have the same right or it's a double standard which I refuse to accept. Infanticide seems to be the word of the day.

As said before, I love babies, small children and animals. Most grown-ups can go to hell as far as I'm concerned because they become hateful and develop traits of lying, stealing, cheating and even killing each other. Being in law enforcement for twenty five years educated me on human behavior and to always expect the unexpected. It got to the point that I didn't have to see death I could smell it. When it came to human behavior nothing ever surprised me because I had seen it all. We just had suicide bombers in a Muslim country overseas blow up three churches killing 300 Christians who were inside praying on Easter Sunday. Then we had some young idiot in South Carolina burn down three churches. In some big cities you can't walk to the store to buy a loaf of bread without someone trying to blow your brains out.

Leave your house and some punk breaks in and steals your valuables. Drive your car and have some moron try to shoot you because you accidently blew the car horn. Go to the store and while you're inside some asshole is breaking into your car. It never ends and you wonder why I love and respect animals more then humans? I have been victimized and hurt by other people my entire life and have yet ever been hurt by an animal.

The one person that I despise even more than a lawyer is the sexual predator like the one I had suing me. Between him and his psychopathic wife I really had my hands full. He is a full blown active sexual predator that has a line of bullshit that he uses on women that makes them believe that he's such a gentleman and nice person. Predators dress and always present themselves as well respected and normal people. They are mentally sick and will resort to anything in order to get into the confidence of a naive female. They are usually married to disguise what they really are and their intentions. Predators know where the fertile fields are and they certainly don't waste their time attending church functions and joining civic groups. You will find them flooding work out gyms because that's where the half dressed women are. He will waste no time in making friends with three or four ladies but he will always target one specific woman that is friendly and obviously naive. She will swallow his line of bullshit hook line and sinker. She becomes impressed hearing him tell her that she's so beautiful she should be a movie star and how he hopes that her husband appreciates her. It all starts out with an innocent cup of coffee after they workout and a continual barrage of bullshit on how beautiful she is. Before long the predator has her in the local and nearby Holiday Inn screwing her brains out. Once he gives her the staff of life she's in love and her husband at home doesn't seem to be that important anymore. In a short period of time and after numerous sexual encounters the predator will have his victim giving him money, flowers, jewelry and all the ass he can handle.

HARD TIMES

To me a workout gym is nothing more than a very popular whore house where you can find all kinds of sexual perverts, predators and people looking for a strange piece of ass.

Sometimes I wonder what the hell they teach in schools. History doesn't seem to be very important and there's not much truth in what they teach. Just for example, there was a question on the tenth grade final exam regarding President Lincoln that the students actually accepted as fact. Name the two people that got shot in the back of their head while sitting in a theater. The answer was President Lincoln in Fords theater and the guy sitting in front of Peewee Herman in an adult movie theater. This is the kind of garbage being taught in history classes and we wonder why the country is going to hell in a hand basket.

Young people of today have no understanding of hard times and how it feels to be poor. Unless they can drive a nice car to school, wear designer clothes and have money in their pocket they aren't satisfied. This may come as news to those poor down trodden school children, but I had to walk to school my family wasn't able to buy the good life for us.

I sure as hell didn't have any money and I carried my lunch in an empty lard bucket. My mother always fixed me a peanut butter and jelly sandwich for my school lunch. She would always try and find an apple or something to put with my sandwich for desert. As a young kid I never knew that we were dirt poor until I heard someone say it. Even hearing it didn't mean much to me because I was living a normal life like all the other kids on a farm. We didn't have all of the good things in life but it never bothered me because I didn't know the difference.

Every time you turn on the television set these days you see that another police officer has been killed. When I was getting close to retirement I had made up my mind that if anyone was going to shoot my ass it would be off a stool at Donkin Donut. Damn if I was going to give some scumbag the opportunity and pleasure of killing me and depriving me of my retirement income. As a shift commander in the North East District of Miami, I had three detectives killed in one night reminding me how fragile life can be. Three good officers gunned down in cold blood by a worthless dirt bag with a shotgun. Two officers were standing in a narrow hallway that provided no protection and the third officer made it out of the hallway and was gunned down before he had a chance to defend himself. The subject ran to a large seagrape bush for cover where he was finally found dead. The incident began when the three officers observed the subject driving an expensive car and parking in front of an apartment house on Collins Avenue. When they went to the subject's apartment and standing in the hallway the first officer was shot from the kitchen window of the apartment. When the other two officers turned to run the subject shot the second officer in the back as the third officer made it outside of the building where he was gunned down.

As for myself I'm sick and damn tired of police officers being murdered and the unbridled trash of caravans invading our country. It's high time for every citizen to arm themselves and carry a firearm on their person. As a civilian I have every intention of arming myself to protect my life. The day that some scroungy bastard tries to pull me out of my truck and assault me is the day his brains will be splattered all over the street. If everyone is armed you'll be surprised to see how polite and courteous people can become. Now when someone bumps into you the asshole will tell you to watch where the hell you're walking in a threatening manner. When the asshole knows that you're armed, instead of giving you some shit and a lot of lip he'll beg your pardon for bumping into you.

Punks and thieves commits assaults and robberies because they know that the average citizen is law abiding and unarmed. As for me it

HARD TIMES

should be open season on the criminal element and no limit on how many you can bag. Leave a package in your car and watch how long before some scumbag enters your car to steal the package. Of course a lawyer for the scumbag will scream to high heaven that it was a clear case of entrapment and the scumbag defendant should be found not guilty and set free. The run of the mill lawyer will no doubt demand that the police compensate his client for what they have done to him.

I've lived and seen some hard times but if the Democrats are successful in making America a Socialistic country hard times will govern everyones life. Right now the people in Venezuela are wiping their ass with their paper money because it's cheaper than toilet paper which sells for over ten dollars a roll. In our congress right now we have one senator that's older than dirt pushing for Socialism and another young female in congress that's pushing for the same thing and she's dumber than a rock. It's obvious that this knot head of a woman is totally ignorant of economics and has no idea what the hell she's talking about. The voters in California deserve the nit wits that they have voted into office. I thought Governor Jerry Brown was a big asshole regarding his position on sanctuary cities but he can't hold a candle compared to the moron now elected as governor.

The present governor really has his head up his ass in an attempt to recycle.

In my humble and justified opinion most lawyers are nothing but professional thieves and that's basically why they run for congress or any political office. Why they get full time wages is beyond me. Most of the time they do nothing but sit on their ass and socialize. The hours that they put in doesn't even amount to part time employment and it should be recognized as such and paid likewise. Every now and then the freeloading assholes will vote themselves a pay raise. At present they get paid $174,000.00 a year plus what else they can steal for a part time job. The only Democrat that I know of that's worth his salt is Joe Mancin of West Virginia. Rumor has it that Nancy Pelosi was voted Miss Grease Rack in her younger days. She looks like she's had her rack greased a few times that's for sure. All the Democrats in the House of Representatives follow her around with their nose in her ass like a bunch of sheep.

The Democrats are scared to death that the Supreme Court Justice Ruth Ginsberg who is 85 years old might die causing President Trump to appoint another Conservative to the Supreme Court. The 20/20 presidential election is going to be a real hum dinger to say the least. We have that newly elected senator that doesn't know her ass from a hole in the ground and is a die hard Socialist. She thinks that something should be done with the cows because they fart too much and pollutes the air with methane gas. If that's the way she feels then the next time she cuts the cheese maybe she should turn herself in to the Environmental Protection Agency. A news flash to the dummy, seven billion people on earth and they are far more guilty of producing methane gas than a bunch of cows. If she had her way they'd make it a felony to fart. Even now if you fart on a crowded elevator in the presence of a lawyer you can expect a subpoena to appear in court.

In these days we have wall to wall lawyers that sue for everything underneath the sun. For example we have one jerk ass lawyer representing some asshole that's suing his parents for not asking him if he wanted to be born. If this idiot really wanted to win the case he would have hired the Grunt and Dump law firm that sued me because those sorry bastards will lie and do whatever possible to win a case. They think nothing of swearing lies on affidavits and finding a judge that will sign anything even after being told that the affidavits are based entirely on perjury. If a disaster occurs any place within the hour you'll have lawyers crawling all over each other signing up clients. In my experience most lawyers that I've come across are anything but professional in their conduct and have no boundaries of decency. Filing false affidavits in court before a judge means nothing to them.

Every now and then I'm reminded of someone that represents the best of people. One case in particular is a 91 year old patriot that devoted his life supporting the American dream. His name is Richard H. Plager, an individual that I worked with on the Dade County Sheriff's Office in Miami, Florida. He spent 37 years in law enforcement with the Miami and Dade County Police. He joined the Miami Police Department in 1950 and retired as a police captain from the Dade County Police Department in 1988. He was Chief of Detectives when E. Wilson Purdy became Director and a difference of opinion developed between them and Mr. Plager became the Chief of Police of Sanibel, Florida and retired again in 1996. Then Mr. Plager went to Israel where he was on the Tourist Police for twelve years. He holds a Masters Degree in Public Administration and served in the military from World War 2 with the United States Navy and retired after 24 years including the Naval Reserve.

Mr. Plager always tried to keep himself informed by reading books. General Patton, one of our country's best allegedly said when he defeated the German General Rommel in a tank battle in North Africa in 1942, "Rommel, you magnificent bastard I read your book."

Everyone that gives a damn should make an effort to at least read the Koran which is the bible of the Muslims and Islam. Their teachings identify the Jews and Christians as infidels and their death will be by fire. What happened to the Twin Towers in America is an example of what they teach. They raise suicide bombers like we raise chickens. They are so ignorant they carry bombs in back packs and walk into churches or any placed packed with people and blow themselves up. Just recently a half dozen of the morons walked into different churches and hotels killing 390 innocent people. They breed like flies and their main goal is to take over the entire world and rid themselves of all infidels once and for all.

Everyone should be reminded that our country was founded by Christians and identified as such until Obama toured the world claiming otherwise. Radical liberals are making every effort to see that America becomes a Socialistic nation but God bless President Trump when he stated during the State of The Union address that America will never become a Socialist nation.

Unfortunately some people are deaf or don't give a rat's ass when President Trump said, "Buy American, Hire American." By the way our so called patriots are buying and driving foreign made cars it's obvious that they're trying to destroy America's automobile industry. Nothing pisses me off more when I see some idiot driving a Toyota with a decal of an American flag stuck on the bumper. I asked one jerk that happens to be in the family why doesn't he buy an American car and he responded when they make a good one I'll buy it. No offense Clyde, but I don't think you have brains enough to understand how to put air in a tire and now you profess to know something about the construction of automobiles?

Every now and then I'm reminded of my youthful days back on the farm in Alabama and wonder how the hell we ever survived. I suppose my biggest blessing was not understanding anything about being poor. Ignorance can be a real blessing in so many ways. It never occurred to me that some houses actually had electric lights and running water in their houses much less and indoor restroom. When I followed my mother in a cotton field picking cotton it didn't strike me as being unusual. Picking cotton and working in the corn fields was just an accepted as a way of life. Some things you never forget like my oldest brother having me stand next to him and fan him to keep him cool and the flies run off. That and my father asking me "if I thought that I would ever amount to anything" as I polished his shoes. In those days neighbors helped each other because outside help didn't exist. You had to literally live off the land or you'd starve to death. Many times I remember being served polk salad for breakfast with biscuits and gravy. My mother did the best she could do with nothing and certainly didn't deserve such a hard life. She cooked on an old wood burning stove and boiled peanuts in an effort to get some cooking oil out of them. She made great jelly out of watermelon rinds, apples and peaches.

When I was a tiny little kid I was scared to go to the outhouse by myself and sometimes I would accidently soil my pants. I'll never forget my oldest sister would walk around the house singing "we're going to hang ole Bobby on the sour apple tree."

If someone got sick in the family there wasn't much you could do about it because there wasn't any kind of medical facility in town or licensed care givers. Having some kind of medicine on hand was unheard of. The nearest hospital was a hundred miles away in Birmingham. The best thing going for a sick person was prayer and plenty of it. People died of rather simple things practically unheard of these days. My mother had a picture of her brother lying in his casket. He use to carry a revolver in his pants pocket and one day as he was taking the gun out of his pocket it discharged striking him in the leg. From that minor gun shot wound he developed gangrene and it killed him.

You never know when your number is up and ail of your plans don't mean anything. The only plan that is important is God's plan. One good example of that is the day I was having coffee with my friend and without saying a word or making a sound he fell over dead.

Is it my imagination or what? Most of the idiot politicians seem to be in or from the state of California. The new governor reminds me of a bowel movement and the best part of him fell into the toilet.

Apparently most of the voters in California are drowning in ignorance and they deserve what they get. You're either well off or you're sleeping in tents or card board boxes on the sidewalks. Each morning crews come out with pressure cleaning equipment to wash the piles of feces and puddles of piss off the sidewalks. Thousands of homeless citizens and illegal immigrants relieving themselves on the sidewalks, streets and any other convenient place they can find. Telephone booths use to be the preferred place to use as a toilet, but now it doesn't seem to matter the sidewalk is good enough.

The Socialist Party also known as the Democratic Party is hell bent on making America another Venezuela. In the large cities in California just be careful where you're stepping otherwise you might step in a feces pie. The Socialist running for president readily admit that they are for open borders and tearing down the existing border wall with Mexico. The candidates don't see the thousands of immigrants invading our country, they only see potential Democratic voters who will support their liberal agenda. For months all the Democratic big whigs said that President Trump manufactured the crisis on the Mexican border but now they are forced to admit that there is a real crisis at the border. Even at that they still won't do anything to help stop the influx of hundreds of thousands of immigrants invading our country. Just one note, if I ever vote for a Democrat a piano will come out of my ass playing "who would have thought it."

If the American people think they've seem some hard times wait until the Democratic Party takes over the government. If the blacks and other people of color think they've had it so bad then be white for awhile and really discover how it feels to be trampled on and blamed for everything. My dislike for lawyers and judges is well known and for good reason. I've never met a lawyer yet that didn't have a goal of screwing someone. If I'm lying I'm dying. Stand on a street corner and fart if you don't believe me. If there's a lawyer within three feet then you can expect a subpoena to appear in court as a defendant for violating a rule with the Environmental Protection Agency.

It's a medical fact that men performing oral sex on the ladies can give them throat cancer. Medical science could never understand why but I am certain that I have discovered the cause and will gladly share it with others even though it prohibits one of the basic joys of life. Since a teenager I have always had a great deal of pride in myself for being recognized as a champion muff diver but many times I would come up with my face covered with a white powder. The next thing I hear is that lawyers representing one woman won a million dollar verdict from the court claiming that the talcum powder caused the woman to develop cancer of the vagina. It doesn't take a rocket scientist to understand why men develop throat cancer. Well hear ye, hear ye and let it be known across the land. For a million dollars I'll sprinkle it on my head and crotch. I'll snort the shit, put it in my coffee and put it on my cereal every morning. Of course with my luck I would probably come down with a severe case of throat cancer before I got a dime.

So far twenty Socialist Democrats have thrown their hats in the ring to run for president in 20/20. Most of them appear to have a vision problem. Their optic nerve seems to be attached to their asshole giving them a shitty outlook on life.

If you're looking for a good liar to represent you I strongly recommend Douche Bag Mary of the Grunt and Dump law firm in Fort Lauderdale, Florida located on West Broward Blvd. This lying bitch has absolutely no scruples and will file a lawsuit against anyone for anything. Fart on an elevator or get caught scratching your ass and she'll file a lawsuit against you. This bitch puts John Dillinger to shame when it comes to robbing people and she does it without a gun. Her specialty is representing trailer trash because she feels more comfortable with her kind of people.

I've lived through some hard times in my life and struggled like hell to have something just to have it taken away by some sorry ass lying douche bag lawyer and a couple brain dead judges. I suspect that more value was placed on a piece of ass then the truth. Hopefully when any of the sorry bastards die they're buried face up with their mouth open because I intend to make their grave sites my personal latrine. The sorry bastards have ruined and destroyed my life and some day they will have to stand good for what they have done. Pay back can be a bitch.

The love of money is the root of all evil so they say. In the past you could buy a television set plug it in, turn it on and watch television. Not so today, now it will cost you an arm and a leg to watch television. A person with a couple television sets can pay as much as two hundred dollars a month to be able to watch television. It's just another way of screwing the public no doubt contrived by a bunch of lawyers for money. Any time I think of someone getting screwed I automatically think of lawyers. In my opinion lawyers are people too damn lazy to actually work and have perfected their ability to live on other peoples money. All of them seem to exhibit an attitude of "holier then thou" toward other people. It may come as a surprise but just because a lawyer becomes a judge certainly doesn't indicate that he or she understands all aspects of the law. During my specific case where I was robbed I appeared before a Superior Court judge that didn't know his ass from a hole in the ground. That moron never even recognized that I was even in the courtroom or even asked me one question. He had my entire written defense on his desk before him even with one of the slanderous posters with my wife's picture which were distributed and posted all over the county by the plaintiff.

The opposing lawyer made the claim that my wife and I had gotten a divorce sometime in the past but didn't submit one document to prove it. He couldn't present one iota of proof and yet the judge accepted his argument and continued to just sit there like a potted plant saying nothing because it was obvious that he didn't know anything about the law regarding "tenants by the entirety." The state law "tenants by the entirety" protects a persons property from someone taking it. My wife and I had renewed our wedding vowels four years before any summary judgment was ever filed against me yet the brain dead judge ruled that we were "tenants in common" permitting our property to be taken from us. The judge signed an order drawn up by the lawyer requesting that the sheriff of the county auction off our house, car, jewelry, furniture, appliances and all of our personal property to pay the summary judgment which was obtained through perjury.

The true and complete story of the trailer trash and their lying ass lawyer is told in the book "Kangaroo Justice And Well Dressed Thieves With A License To Steal." Read how some trash can publish and distribute slanderous posters about someone and have the slandered person forced to pay them $125,000.00 for doing it. Then you will understand why I say the Rule of Law sucks big time.

It always amazes me that most readers enjoy reading make believe stories and fictional people. For myself I don't waste my time on make believe people when there are so many assholes to write about. Sometime I always see myself in that song Eddie Arnold sings "Make the world go away and take it off my shoulders because this time Lord you've given me a mountain that I may never be able to climb." That was exactly the way I felt when my first wife was divorcing me and threatening to take my little boy from me. The straw that broke the camel's back was when she told me that "I made her skin crawl." Little did I know that she had been giving her ass away to relatives and other family members. I gave her two options regarding our marriage. One, she could get a divorce giving up custody of my son and move on with her sex hungry life or two, divorce me, take my son and be killed. Fortunately for her she chose option one. It seems like my life is just one mountain after another. I was always reminded of my pathetic young life on that run down farm back in Alabama.

No wonder why my dad would always ask me if I was ever going to amount to anything? It may be hard to believe by some people but I never knew that I was poor until we moved to Miami and I heard someone say it. Most of the young people of today have never experienced hard times of being without and probably can't even spell it.

From the time we moved to Miami, Florida in the back of a coal truck nothing came easy for my dear mother. Simply put, if she's not an angel in heaven then there's no heaven. As a young man I found my mother dead on her living room floor which I still haven't gotten over to this day. A word of advice to everyone. Don't let a day go by without telling your parents and loved ones that you love them. If the words come hard to you then that's even more reason why you should say it. My family consisted of nine and I'm the only one left living. When a love one dies you will always recall every mean and hurtful word that you ever said to them. I would give everything I have if I could only hug and tell my mother how much I love her one more time.

I have already purchased myself a grave site, funeral and headstone because I know that my time on this earth is running out. Needless for anyone other than myself to understand but I find it comforting to place flowers on my own grave site. I always wanted to buy my wife and I a newer car before I kick the bucket because ours is twenty four years old with 300,000 miles on it. Due to the lying bitch lawyer in Broward County Florida and two brain dead judges I have been ruined financially and ever getting a newer car is out of the question. At least I'll get to ride in the back of a nice hearse on the way to the cemetery when I die. The legal system, lawyers and two careless judges completely destroyed my life and apparently enjoyed doing it. Some day the sorry bastards will have to stand good before God at the Pearly Gates for what they have done to me and other innocent people victimized by them in the name of justice.

HARD TIMES

They remind me of how a septic tank works. I'm not a student of how a septic tank functions but I do know that the biggest lumps always seems to float to the top. In most organizations including some police departments that's how some employees get to the top. I served twenty five years with a police department in Miami, Florida and having ability and being qualified had nothing to do with being promoted to top supervisory positions. Most organizational charts reminds me of piles of shit being thrown against the wall. I retired from what was once a kick ass police department but it slowly evolved into a kiss ass police department. Promotions within the department turned into one big ass kissing contest. To hell with taking a promotional exam just kiss the right ass and you'll be one of the boys. During my tenure with the Dade County Sheriff's Office I saw people getting promoted to supervisory positions that appeared not to have completed the sixth grade in elementary school. Some recruits were actually being taught how to read and write while being employed by the Sheriff's Office.

Don't label a person with some derogatory label unless you know that it's true. Imagine someone saying big woman, big pussy and little woman all pussy. Logic alone tells you that it's not true and shouldn't be said. I personally take offense to it because I've been a muff diver since I was a teenager and it's absolutely not true and anyone saying it should be ashamed and have their mouth washed out with soap.

Sometimes life can be frightening because you never know when your number on earth is up. Life is so fragile and unpredictable it has a way of making a person feel that they're skating on thin ice. The Lord never promised us one day so live each day as though it was your last. Just recently a large crane fell off the top of a building under construction and killed four people on the ground. Two people just sitting in their car were crushed to death so take life with a grain of salt.

I never dreamed in my entire life that people would accept murdering unborn and born babies like they are doing today. Infanticide doesn't seem to bother a lot of people to my disbelief. It's simply murder and if you call it anything else then you have your head up your ass. I'm not a fan of Russian President Vladimir Putin, but I strongly agree with him when he says that everyone should not be entitled to a trial. When someone like a serial killer or some slimy bastard that abducts and kills some innocent child. When the sorry bastard admits to it and the evidence is over whelming the bastard should be executed by a family member of the victim. It pisses me off royally to see some murdering bastard get sentenced to a long term in prison for the tax payers to support and take care of. The scumbag should be executed and his organs given to good law abiding citizens. What's left of him should be donated to the zoo to help feed the animals. Lethal injection sucks when it comes to executing the bastard. Murdering bastards should be drawn and quartered or hung in the public square until they rot. Everyone has a shit list of people that have done them wrong and tried to destroy their lives. The list has no boundaries and is comprised of people from all walks of life. My particular list contains a superior court judge in North Carolina, a circuit court judge in Fort Lauderdale, Florida, a lying douche bag lawyer in Plantation, Florida, a young lawyer in Asheville, North Carolina and a trailer trash couple in Plantation, Florida. The douche bag lawyer wears lying and perjury as a badge of honor and thinks nothing of bending over to get an affidavit signed. She works with her husband and another relative in the Grunt and Dump law firm in West Broward County Florida and he has to be dumb as a rock to not see what's going on with a judge and her sexual predator and trailer trash client that she represents. That sorry ass bitch knows who I'm talking about and I hope she rots in hell where she belongs. If the bitch ever dies I'll make the 800 mile trip down there to take a dump on her grave to show her that there's no hard feelings.

Not to beat a dead horse but the Superior Court judge in North Carolina was nothing more than a potted plant that didn't know his ass from a hole in the ground regarding the state law that protects a person's home and property. During the entire hearing the only thing

I heard him say was to the lawyer, "draw up the order and I'll sign it." If that asshole and indifferent judge had any sense of justice and fair play a piano will come out of my ass again playing "who would have thought it." The unconcerned asshole was wrong then, he is still wrong today and he'll be wrong tomorrow until his incompetent ass is stuck in his grave.

Someone please tell me why some too lazy to work moron goes to law school and comes out thinking they're smarter than everyone else on earth? Most lawyers that I've come across couldn't hit their own ass with a bow fiddle. It seems that their goal in life is to hold public office so they can sit on their ass do nothing and get paid for it.

Sometimes I wonder what the hell they're teaching kids in school these days. Ask any kid if they have ever heard of Patrick Henry or Nathan Hale and they'll just give you a blank look. In high school we were taught that Patrick Henry was a great statesman that supported the American revolution and shouted those famous and unforgettable words in Virginia as he held a sword high, "I know not what course others may take but as for me I'll take intercourse." Wait a minute, I've been told that my memory has failed me and I've been corrected. He actually said, "I know not what course others may take but as for me, give me liberty or give me death." That sounds much better and I was in high school 65 years ago and I can understand why my memory failed me.

At least I'm positive about Nathan Hale when he was standing on an English gallow waiting to be hung and said, "I only regret that I have but one life to give for my country." Now watch someone correct me and say that he was known to be hung real good but it didn't have a thing to do with death. As you grow old you will find that your memory will fail you so be careful when you quote someone.

At present they have discovered a scandal involving how wealthy people get their kids into well known colleges by paying off particular people that are attached to the college. They make large donations to the school, falsify records, cheat on the Sat exams and anything else to get admitted into the schools. While deserving people are standing in line to be admitted into a school, parents with money and influence have their kids enter through the back door.

I have taken the Sat examination myself to enter a college and it takes two hours and better to complete. In my opinion there's not a person on the planet that can make a perfect score without cheating. Many of the questions are so complicated and in depth that they're difficult to even understand. It's my understanding that Senator Chuck Schumer the minority leader in the U.S. Senate made a perfect score on his Sat examination. For myself I'd like to know which college Mr. Schumer was applying for and if he had any assistance in taking the exam. Could it be possible that Mr. Schumer entered the college through the back door like the other cheaters?

Like I've said before, there's a time to be happy and a time to be sad, a time to laugh and a time to cry but the most important saying is that there's a time to live and a time to die. Sometimes it seems like the hard times of my life just won't go away. It certainly doesn't seem like I'm on the highway to heaven that's for sure. If anyone thinks that they are protected by defamation laws then they had better think again. My family was slandered to high heaven by a trailer trash couple that gave new meaning to freeloading. They have perfected the art of ripping off the system to the point of writing a book about how to do it and get away with it. The husband is a sexual predator and his wife is a psychopath who spends her time following him around to see what woman he's picking up. If you're interested in seeing exactly what justice is worth read the book "Kangaroo Justice And Well Dressed Thieves With A License To Steal." All it takes is a lying ass bitch lawyer and two incompetent asshole judges and with little effort they can destroy your life.

HARD TIMES

What the hell has happened to the America that I grew up in? Maybe I'm wrong but I don't think so because I'm under the opinion that William Shakespeare had it right when he said that "we need to round up all the lawyers and get rid of them." People in congress sit on their ass most of the time doing nothing worth while and get paid for doing it. Why the hell don't people wake up? It's a part time job and should be treated and paid for in that manner. If their salaries were cut in half they'd still be over paid for what they do. When Rand Paul was running for office I donated $50.00 for his campaign. The way he refused with eleven other Republicans to support President Trump on the national emergency I would appreciate it if he would return my donation so I can give it to President Trump.

When I first became a police officer it didn't take me long to realize that a lot of people were under the impression that my ass was a football. Being physically abused was so routine that I went back and checked the job description of a police officer to see if getting my ass kicked was an accepted part of the job description.

It seems like my life has just been one mountain after another and the easy life was never in sight. As a young boy in the cotton and corn fields of Alabama the future of climbing up the ladder of success appeared hopeless. My father asked me many times if I thought that I would ever amount to anything? All I can say is "I tried to dad but it just didn't work out." I went to colleges and got a good education but I could never reach the top of the mountain as hard as I tried. It seemed like I was never at the right place at the right time and knew the right people.

I personally feel that things are going to get so bad in our country that I'm always reminded of what Plato once said. I've quoted him before but it's so true and important that it's worth saying it again until it's buried in your mind. "The attitudes of the citizens and programs carried to such extreme that even the little puppy dogs in our house holds will rise up on their hind legs and demand their rights.

The situation and turmoil will grow so bad that the government will hire anyone that can restore order." Even now a white person has to apologize for being white.

This particular point of view that I'm going to express will certainly label me as a racist but it's true whether people like it or not. If I was of African decent I would thank God every day for slavery in colonial times otherwise I would probably be in Africa running around with a spear looking for something to eat. At the time slavery was an accepted practice in the South and throughout other countries for a thousand years so don't get bent out of shape over it. Just a tid bit of information for the ignorant regarding the war between the states. The war was for Southern independence and not over slavery. It was a simple case of Southern people being taxed without representation. President Lincoln made it a war over slavery when it became quite clear to him that the Northern people were getting tired of the war. Lincoln issued the Emancipation Proclamation in order to stir up some interest in the war.

Whatever happened to the saying that President Trump made regarding "hire American, buy American?" The American people are only interested in what directly effects them. Most are about as patriotic as a fart snapper in the bathtub. They will attend a campaign rally or sporting event, sing the national anthem and wave the American flag like there's no tomorrow. Oh, they are so proud of America but when the event is over 90% of them will drive home in their foreign made vehicles. They are either ignorant as hell or simply don't give a tinkers damn about destroying the American automotive industry. It's a real joke to see a decal of an American flag on the bumper of a Toyota or any other foreign made vehicle. Maybe it's the owners way of showing his patriotism and making him feel good.

General Motors is closing down a plant in Ohio as a result of so called patriotic citizens not buying Chevrolets and a demanding union. Just an example of what foreign car buyers are doing to our country.

HARD TIMES

Foreign car companies can and do avoid paying tariffs by simply exporting their cars in pieces and assembling them in America.

Life sure as hell is not fair. Take the case of the man that builds bridges his entire life and he's never recognized as a bridge builder but let him suck just one cock and he'll always be known as a cock sucker.

No doubt everyone has had their trials and tribulations during their life time. It just seems like the ghost of hard times has followed me around through no fault of mine. For example the following is one of the letters that I wrote to Circuit Court Judge Haury of Fort Lauderdale, Florida regarding a lying ass female lawyer that has harassed me for twenty years. The only thing changed in the letter is the lawyer's name which will be Douche Bag Mary.

June 20, 2013

Dear Judge Haury:

I just received your ruling on the above case number and quite frankly I'm floored in disbelief. How can someone be slandered and humiliated for years and then have someone destroy their lives as effectively as blowing their brains out with a gun?

Is this the way our system of justice is suppose to work? I have done everything that the court has ordered and the harassment never ends. From the very beginning of Douche Bag Mary's campaign of harassment started she has never been obligated to prove anything. Whatever she alleges is accepted as truth and nothing else seemed to matter.

I don't understand to this day how she manages to get injunctions against me without having any basis for doing so. It might be of interest to her to know that another Robert Elliott resides in Buncombe County, North Carolina and I'm not the only one with that name. It's obvious that she has me confused with the other Robert Elliott if it makes any difference to her.

Would you believe it? I have been harassed and sued for the past 15 years because I objected to her plaintiffs posting slanderous signs all over town with my wife's picture claiming that she's nothing more than a sexually diseased whore. Douche Bag Mary knows that my wife and I can't travel due to our health and financial problems and she uses it to get whatever she wants by default.

Your ruling has destroyed my life, how much I have left, which I suspect isn't that much. My cries for help were never heard by anyone and it seemed that everyone couldn't careless. I have been wronged big time. Our peace of mind has been destroyed along with our lives.

I mow yards instead of filing for unemployment and I don't fake an injury to get a disability nor do I get food stamps. I can't bring myself to be a freeloader like millions of other people. Too often I have a choice when I go to the pharmacy for medicine. I can eat or buy medicine, usually I opt to eat. So often I can't buy my medication or my wife's and now I have to pay over $150,000.00 to the people that have destroyed our lives?? Considering that, then there's not much left.

At night when I lay myself down to sleep, if I should die before I wake I pray the Lord my soul to take. No one can take that from me.

Yours truly,

Robert Elliott

HARD TIMES

Hopefully the judge can sleep at night knowing that he accepted an affidavit based solely on perjury that he was told about on two separate occasions by the author.

Anytime you hear a person and especially a politician use the word progressive be careful who you support. Every progressive group or organization that I've ever known was totally controlled and dominated by radicals. A typical example would be the moron that always runs around town with his greasy hair on fire yelling "no justice, no peace." I would guess that the best part of that idiot ran down his momma's leg. Years ago when I was with the Dade County Sheriffs Office I had to run his ass out of the police station for creating a disturbance at the front desk. At the time he was a fat ass with long hair and a mustache. Years never changed him because he still looks as stupid to this day. As I was kicking his fat ass out of the police station I'll never forget what he said. "If a humming bird had any brains it could fly backwards." I've never been able to figure out the logic in such a stupid statement but with him 2 plus 3 always equaled 6. It's well known that you can't fix stupid so I suppose his answer will always be 6.

Have you ever seen such an accumulation of assholes running for president on the Democratic Socialist ticket? That much stupidity in one room could be disastrous for the country.

As a result of Obamacare the medical insurance premiums for my wife went from $189.00 a month to $456.00 a month. I couldn't pay the high premiums and had to drop the insurance coverage. This year when filing my 2018 Federal taxes I was penalized over $1,600.00 for not having insurance on my wife. As for me they can stick Obama care up their ass. Between the lying ass lawyers, brain dead judges and Obama, I don't think I'll ever be able to dig myself out of a hole.

STORY

With my luck I figured that my final resting place would probably be a commercial dumpster behind Wal-Mart or some other place. Every time I turn around I'm confronted with another problem and it seems like hard times never ends for me. Why can't goodness and mercy come my way just once. Every adventure I ever started in an effort to get on easy street failed including writing books. I spent hundreds of dollars advertising my books on line with companies like Barnes and Nobles and Amazon to no avail. The only way to successfully sell books is to get them in stores so the buying public can see them. I don't know what it takes or what I have to do but come hell or high water I'll get them in stores if it's the last thing I ever do. They say that freedom isn't free. Well take it from me neither is life.

My mind always drifts back to my youth on that farm in Alabama. I never knew what it was to wear store bought clothes or actually own a leather Winter jacket. Every time I hear Dolly Parton sing about her coat of many colors that her mother made for her, I'm reminded of the clothes that my mother made for me out of empty flour sacks. I had four older brothers and I always wore hand me down clothes from them even as a teenager. It never bothered me being poor because I didn't understand what it meant to be poor. To me everyone was all alike and no one was better or worse then anyone else. The reality of it all didn't hit me until as a young boy in school I heard my first grade teacher Mrs. McCormick, tell her son that I was poor.

Occasionally I tell something humorous while writing in order to over ride the sad part of my life. Some people have a one track mind when they're told something whether true or not it becomes imbedded in their mind. For example, a mother tells her young teenager son a falsehood about girls in order to keep him from getting into trouble when he starts recognizing and being attracted to the girls. The mother makes an absurd statement that a girl's vagina has teeth and convinces her son that it's true and under no circumstances should he ever indulge in sex. As the young man grew into manhood his long time girl friend finally asked him why he never seemed interested in having sex with her. He explained to her that his mother had told him that a woman's vagina had teeth and not to have anything to do with it. His girl friend laughed and said that she had never heard anything so ridiculous and immediately exposed herself to him for examination stating "see there's no teeth" to which he responded "of course not, look at the condition of those gums." Sometimes a little humor reminds me that all of life doesn't have to be gloom and doom. Always try and remember if you find yourself in a rut it's nothing but a grave open at both ends.

One of the greatest inventions to ever come along is the mute button on the remote control of the television set. Being a cripple I spend a lot of time watching television and nothing gags me more than have to watch the same commercials over and over again. Everything is always advertised at whatever and 99 cents. The marketing genius knows that if it's advertised at $20.99 the customer will always tell everyone that he only paid $20.00 for the item. It's just another marketing technique playing on ignorance.

As I get older I'm convinced that hard times will be with me until the day I kick the bucket. It has gotten to the point that I have absolutely no respect for lawyers and judges. I was born dirt poor and accepted poverty as a way of life but never knew how evil and mean people could be until I reached manhood. As a result of a Summary lawsuit being filed against me by a lying bitch lawyer on behalf of some trailer trash I have more respect and love for animals then I do for most human beings. I previously reproduced a letter that I had written to a circuit court judge in Fort Lauderdale, Florida on June 20, 2013 regarding the actions of a female lawyer in his district that was unable to know the difference between a lie and the truth. After receiving more letters from the dumb ass lawyer I wrote the judge again on August 26, 2013 regarding her delusional attitude. The following is the exact letter and the only thing changed is the lawyer's name which has been changed to read Douche Bag Mary.

August 26, 2013

Dear Judge Haury:

I just received a letter from Douche Bag Mary informing me that a hearing has been scheduled for September 3, 2013 at 8:45 a.m. to determine if I should be held in contempt of court for not filling out papers for something that I don't know anything about. If I had opened an account someplace I'd be glad to fill out the information but like I've said before it's quite impossible to supply information about something that I know absolutely nothing about.

On the first judgment against me I was charged with willfully and knowingly violating a court order that I didn't know anything about and she even admitted that I was never notified and by law she didn't have to notify me. That's nice, a person can be held responsible for something that he knows absolutely nothing about.

The latest lawsuit is even better than that. She accuses me of opening an account someplace in her client's names. I have never opened any kind of account in my life and did borrow money from my wife's credit card to get our house out of foreclosure and that's the only time I ever had to borrow money.

I wrote you a letter in my defense asking you or anyone else to provide me with any information regarding the mysterious account that I was being accused of opening. The request was also made to Douche Bag Mary and she refused to provide any information. Is it unfair to ask that Douche Bag Mary produce the papers of the account that she accuses me of opening just to see whose signatures appear on the papers and who received any money? Some effort should have been made to determine who opened the account before another person's life is destroyed by a bunch of lies. Douche Bag Mary knows full well that it's quite impossible for me to drive to Florida to appear in court due to my health and lack of money for expenses. The reason that Douche Bag Mary submitted the papers for me to fill out within 45 days is simply because I have no idea what she's talking about.

Douche Bag Mary has been trying to shake me down anyway that she can for the past 10 years and quite frankly I don't see any end to it.

Yours truly,

Robert L. Elliott

Judge Haury never showed me the respect to even acknowledge my letters and only exhibited a cool attitude of indifference.

In desperation I wrote the following letter to Mr. Mark Pinston of the Van Winkle law firm on June 8, 2016 to find out if lying under oath and being a false witness would have any impact on a case. Why shouldn't a lawyer be disbarred permanently from practicing law and their license revoked for committing perjury?

June 8, 2016

Dear Mr. Mark Pinston:

I have some legal problems that I need some help with before a Florida lawyer completely destroys what life I have left.

STORY

In 1998 I sued a trailer trash couple here in Asheville for distributing hundreds of slanderous posters with my wife's picture on them stating that she was nothing more than a diseased whore and anyone having anything to do with her should report to the Health Clinic for treatment. They even posted signs on the front door of our church house and all our neighbors including shopping centers. I reported it to the Buncombe County police department and the trailer trash fled town and went to South Florida for the wife to avoid talking to the police. The husband admitted to the police that he had a picture of my wife but had given it to his wife. Shortly thereafter slanderous posters started appearing all over town with my wife's picture on them.

I sued them for slander in a local court here in Asheville and a judgment was placed against them for $35,000.00 which I never made an effort to collect. When almost 10 years had gone by I thought I'd go ahead and renew the judgment considering what they had done to our reputation.

Shortly after renewing the judgment with a local attorney Biggers, I was informed by Mr. Biggers that he was informed by the trailer trash that the judgment had been satisfied in 2003 by a court order from a bankruptcy court in Broward County, Florida which my wife and I knew nothing about. I called their attorney Douche Bag Mary and asked her why didn't she notify us of their bankruptcy that satisfied the judgment and she told me that under Florida law she was obligated to notify me of anything. I told her that we should have been notified by her or her clients and not doing so was inexcusable on their part.

The next thing I know she filed a lawsuit against me for of all things "willfully and knowingly violating a court order" which was completely untrue and a lie that she admitted to me in proud fashion. Even at that the Broward County Court accepted the lawsuit after being informed that it was based completely on a lie. The court set a court date and I immediately wrote the court and told them that it was impossible for me to appear and asked for time due to having a very mentally ill son that I had to find someone to care for and enough time to try and borrow money to make the trip because I was financially unable to make such a trip at that time. I simply had to have time to get up the money to appear.

Apparently the judge couldn't care less about my problems and held court anyway and placed a $151,865.00 judgment against me. I was denied my day in court which every citizen is entitled to with complete disregard of my rights.

I finally hired a local attorney here in Asheville to file bankruptcy for me because of my failing health and being in a position where it was beginning to be impossible to pay all of my and my wife's medical bills. Especially her insurance premiums which kept going up. Since their lawyer Douche Bag Mary, started suing me for everything she can think of for the past 20 years I have had two heart attacks as well as two strokes and the last stroke took my vision in my left eye and my right leg from the knee down is paralyzed and I have to use a walker to get around.

Now of all things their lawyer has filed a summary judgment against me here in Asheville using the Van Winkle law firm. That law firm has done everything they can think of to assist the Florida lawyer to destroy what life I have left. With all my medical problems and being 82 years old on my birthday I don't think I'll be around too long. The judgment against me now is around $171,000.00 because they raised the interest rate from 4.75% to 8% for some reason.

I hired a Mr. Edward Hay to file bankruptcy which satisfied their judgment against me but the summary judgment filed against me and upheld by the court here in Asheville just placed it against me again. My lawyer didn't hesitate to tell me that he wasn't happy being on the case and would like for it to be over. Can you give me a ball park figure what an appeal on the summary judgment would cost? Is there someway I can fight the judgment and prevent the lawyers from taking my personal property? I don't have much and even my car is 21 years old and spends a lot of time in the garage being repaired.

I still feel that I'm entitled to a new trial where I can have my day in court.

Thank you for your time and consideration.

Robert L. Elliott

Needless to say I never received a response from any of my letters which tells me that none of them give a damn about that fictitious thing called truth and justice. After living life I'm convinced that the first thing that forms on a fetus is the asshole and the rest grows on it to form a baby. During my career in law enforcement I worked in the General Investigations Unit for years and gained a lot of knowledge in the area of sexual offenses. If I was looking for a sexual predator the first place I'd go to find one is the local gym where everyone goes to work out. Some of those places serve as a whore house where unhappy and horny men and women congregate. It's the best place in the world to find ass and a sexual predator on the prowl. It's the perfect way to legitimize a whore house. In the old days a whore house wasn't advertised and they were constantly changing locations. I've said it before and it needs to be repeated often until it's every woman's bible. Never assume that just because a man wears a coat and tie that it makes him an honorable gentleman that respects women.

HARD TIMES

Sexual predators present themselves as soft spoken and polite gentlemen who are usually married to unsuspecting wives. Married or single their ultimate goal is to target some naive woman and dazzle her with caring bullshit. Always bear in mind that men will lie, steal, cheat and even kill for a strange piece of ass. It's an insatiable appetite that they can't control. Girls at an early age should be educated on male behavior and what they're capable of and what to be aware of because it can save their life.

When it comes to politics no family is immune from ignorance and stupidity. For myself I'm totally convinced that being a lawyer should disqualify anyone from holding public office. A good example is the United States Congress. That place is packed with almost nothing but lawyers and look how they have messed up the country. They all ran for public office so they can sit on their ass and do nothing while drawing a big salary. Now that I look at all of the weirdos running for president on the Democratic ticket I get a severe case of irritated bowel syndrome. It seems like I'm flushing their brains down the toilet and the only cure is for me to stop looking at and hearing them. It's the same feeling that I get when I think of the trailer trash and their lying bitch of a lawyer that ripped me off. That crew and a couple asshole care less judges can pick you clean as a chicken and there's not a damn thing you can do about it. They have you by the short hairs and you can scream until the sky falls in and nothing will change.

I can understand people wanting to get ahead in life but not like what was going on in the court system. In my opinion the only way some court officers were signing sworn affidavits was because they were getting some head. Getting some head and getting ahead might mean two different things to a common layman but apparently not to a court officer.

Some people are always wishing for something. My advice to them is for them to wish in one hand, shit in the other and see which one

STORY

gets filled up first. If most things I see today ever come true "a piano will come out of my ass again playing who would have thought it." Some people really run things into the ground. My father had a way of administering discipline to me and my older brother. Sometimes we would get into a fight and dad always had a way of settling it. He would give a shovel to both of us and tell us to start digging a hole about 20 feet apart and keep digging until he told us to stop. He would sit on a chair and watch us as he smoked a cigarette. After a couple hours of digging the holes looked like craters and then dad would tell me to take my dirt and put it in my brother's hole. And then he'd tell my brother to bring his dirt over to my hole and fill my hole up. He would always explain to us that since we had enough energy to fight each other then we would use that energy to dig holes in the yard.

There were times that I wished that I was back in Alabama working a corn field instead of digging a hole in our back yard. It seems like success has always eluded me in my endeavors to accomplish something.

It bugs the hell out of me to hear of someone being murdered and the police gets the subjects DNA and years go by without the subject being identified. To me there's no excuse for it. Every new born baby should have it's DNA taken and everyone entering the United States including every citizen in the country. There should be national data banks regarding DNA and finger prints for every person in the country. Of course every civil liberties organization in the country will scream like hell but let them scream to hell and back. If we have those two national data banks then getting away with murder where the police has DNA and finger print evidence would make it almost impossible to commit the perfect murder.

The big whigs in the Democratic Party did everything they could do to frame President Trump and have him thrown out of office but it didn't work and now it's going to bite them on the ass. The public including myself never dreamed that our government was so corrupt. Hillary and everyone else in the Democratic Party thought that Hillary had it in the bag and all she did was run around the country smiling and waving to everyone. No one including smiling Hillary could believe it when she lost. If she had won the election we would never have found out how utterly corrupt our government was. Quite frankly I'm suspicious of Mueller, the special counselor on why he took so long even after finding that there was no collusion between President Trump and the Russian government. It appears that he was bound and determined to find the question of obstruction which he was unable to do. As the old saying goes "truth will set you free." Thank God we have a president that places country over politics. It would be appropriate and fitting if a campaign was started to have the image of him placed on Mount Rushmore because he saved our country from becoming a Socialist country lead by a bunch of ignorant Democrats. The Socialist Democratic Party has nothing positive to offer to our country and their drunken days are numbered. There's a true saying and it certainly applies to the leadership of the Democratic Party, "you can't fix stupid."

When you think that things are bad for you and you start feeling bad for yourself, look to other people and you'll discover that you never had it so good. Three years ago I had back surgery and it left me a cripple. I developed diabetic neuropathy and my right leg from the knee down and foot is nothing but dead weight and has stayed swollen since my surgery. I'm unable to walk without a walker and the damaged nerves in my back has also effected my balance. As much as I've tried to be upbeat and appreciate what I have left at times it can be depressing. There are times that I have considered and really thought about having my leg amputated from the knee down and be fitted with an artificial leg. Then maybe I would be able to walk normally and the pain and dead weight of my leg and foot would be gone.

STORY

We had the Kentucky Derby on November 4, 2019 and even a moron should be able to see that something was rotten in Denmark when the winner Maximum Security was disqualified for so-called bumping another horse. It took the entire executive board of the track twenty minutes to make the decision. There wasn't a clear picture of the alleged bumping and bear in mind that bumping is usually accidental and has been going on since the beginning of horse racing. They declared Country House the winner and it certainly stirs an inquiring mind. Hundreds of people bet on Maximum Security to win and only a very few people bet on Country House which would certainly influence the track's decision in not having to pay out a huge amount of money. No winner in the history of the Kentucky Derby has ever been disqualified and the horses have routinely bumped each other dozens of times. There was six million dollars bet on Maximum Security and five hundred dollars bet on Country House which explains why Maximum Security was disqualified by the track. Why the fans aren't raising holy hell is beyond me. The track cheated the best horse out of it's win and hopefully someone will expose what they have done to avoid paying out millions of dollars.

Have you ever tried to do something to dig yourself out of poverty just to be faced with failure? I have numerous times and each time I was tempted to stop trying. The last venture was book writing which I didn't know the first thing about or the great expense involved. I would never advise anyone to undertake book writing unless they're financially set because the cost of getting a book published and on the market it will run roughly $3,500.00. Just publishing the book on line will not get the job done. To be successful the book has to be displayed in stores where the shopping public can see it. I personally feel that the book's cover and title is what attracts attention to it. If it doesn't attract attention it won't sell. The trick of getting your book displayed in stores requires a lot of effort and money.

HARD TIMES

What is so discouraging to a new and unknown author is trying to get his book out on the market for everyone to see. I'm a big fan of Fox News and it seems like every week someone has written a book and it's being displayed and talked about on the news program daily. By the following week they're claiming that it's a best seller. Can you imagine what it would cost an unknown author to have his book advertised on Fox News? I contacted one well known that has a radio show and his charge for advertising something was $6,000.00 a minute. You can pay big money to have your book advertised on line with large book companies but don't hold your breath waiting to see it advertised.

When I'm finally finished I will have a total of four books published and put on the market for a total cost of approximately $14,000.00. I certainly won't get free advertising on Fox News and will be lucky to get back $14.00 for all my effort. It's just another mountain of hard times that I must climb in my life. Sometimes I think of the singer Eddie Arnold who had a song that fit my life so good. "Make the world go away and take it off my shoulders because this time Lord you've given me a mountain that I may never be able to climb." I don't write fiction or make believe stories and people. The four books that will be published are:

1) Kangaroo Justice and Well Dressed Thieves With a License to Steal
2) Roadside Justice
3) America, Love It or Get The Hell Out.
4) Hard Times

Some how and in some way I'm going to find a way of digging myself out of poverty. Life ain't easy and it sure as hell hasn't been easy for me. I always managed to be at the wrong place at the wrong time. Don't fall into the trap of listening to other people's unqualified advice. Listen to your own heart and know that you can do it. Stand up, brush yourself, look the world in the eye and tell all of the non-believers in you to go to hell. Don't look back, look straight ahead and if you have to run over some assholes to reach your goal then do it. Always protect yourself and like the crime world says "keep your friends close but your enemies closer.

I dated a lot of good looking gals in my life time but there was never anyone that could compare to Big Bertha. She was so tall that when we stood toe to toe my nose was in it and if we stood nose to nose my toes was in it. The only time that it really mattered was when we were dancing because it was hard keeping up with the rhythm of the music when my nose was in it. I even took dance lessons at the Arthur Murray Dance Studio and discovered that I have two left feet. I live on my memories of growing up in Miami, Florida during the 50's and 60's. Those good days are gone forever and times have changed to the point that there's no going back. It's a completely different world now and the good old days are gone forever.

In high school we'd go on beach parties in the evenings, build a camp fire and have a wonderful time enjoying each others company. Some Saturday nights we'd go to the hotels on the beach at Collins Avenue and enjoy the entertainment in the hotel basements. I always looked forward to the high school football games between the Miami Edison Red Raiders, the Miami Jackson Generals and the Miami High School Stingrays. Those high school games would draw as many as 40,000 people which is unheard of today.

Needless to say this is the last book that I intend to write because quite frankly it is a lesson dealing in hard times. Trying to advertise and selling a book is a hopeless project for an unknown author. As mentioned before it seems like everyone appearing on Fox News has written a book usually about themselves and their climb up the ladder. They're always given the opportunity to show their book during a program and talk about it for five minutes or so. Within a week or

HARD TIMES

so they will say that it's a best seller with the New York Times. Can you imagine some poor slob writer getting that kind of free national advertisement? I'm an unknown rogue writer that violates all of the standard rules of writing because I don't hesitate to identify an asshole when I see one. If I had to depend on selling a book to eat I'd starve to death in short order. A published writing is the only way a dead man can talk from the grave to let people understand what he was all about.

If you don't remember anything else don't forget this. Be good to all the people you meet on your way up the ladder of success because you're going to meet them again on your way back down. There are some things that happens in your life that you never forget. I'm an old man of 84 years and still remember some shit as though it just happened yesterday. As a new and young police officer I was in a courtroom testifying against a person that I had arrested for larceny. The defendant's lawyer asked me if I had ever stole anything in my life and I answered yes which seemed to surprise everyone in the courtroom including the judge and the lawyer. At that the lawyer stated "by all means please tell the jury what you stole."

I told the judge and jury that my family was very poor when I was eight years old and we lived in a one car garage with a dirt floor. We moved there from a broken down farm in Alabama in back of a coal miner's truck. My mother gave me some stamps out of a ration book that was issued to us during World War 2 and told me to walk to Williams Grocery Store and get a bag of sugar for us. When I got to the store and looking for the sugar I walked pass a vegetable counter and before my eyes was the most beautiful peanuts that I had ever seen. Being hungry I just couldn't resist and reached up on the counter and took a handful of those beautiful peanuts. A man wearing a white apron and working in the store saw what I had done and told me to put the peanuts back and not to steal things.

When I got home I told my mother that I got caught trying to steal some peanuts and with a broken heart I asked if Jesus would forgive me. With tears in her eyes my mother hugged me and told me that Jesus and her would always love me and not to worry. I told the judge that those few little peanuts had bothered me for my entire life. The judge had to dismiss the jury and the entire courtroom until order could be restored.

As soon as I finish this book and get it published I'm going full steam ahead to get all of my books displayed in stores somehow so the shopping public can see them. It's a simple matter that people won't buy what they don't or can't see. An author's life blood is marketing and if he doesn't have it or can't get it then his efforts and dreams will whither and die.

Like I've said before I'm a rogue writer and some people will be offended by my raw humor. If they're that thin skinned they shouldn't be reading the book in the first place. They are probably the same people that wants me to apologize for being white. A news flash for those morons. Old white men sacrificed everything created America whether you like it or not. Thousands of young and old white men gave their lives defending America and saving your worthless ass.

Plato had it right but maybe you confuse Plato with Pluto. You need to take your head out of your ass and wake up to reality. When things like the Democratic Party continue to deteriorate it will become so bad that what Plato predicted will come true. Conditions will change like it did in Nazi Germany like it did prior to World War 2. If you think that it can't happen here in America then you fall into the ranks of stupidity just like the Democratic Party leadership. When it occurs you assholes will start to believe in God and the hereafter but it'll be too late.

HARD TIMES

In Asheville, North Carolina we have a class of misfits that we identify as C.A.V.E. people. Citizens Against Virtually Everything. They are obviously retarded and most conduct themselves like trash. They think nothing of sitting around in front of the police station exposing themselves with tattoos and sagging naked tits that hang so low they look like a couple nuts. The police just stand around gawking at them and doing nothing about it because apparently being obscene doesn't violate any local laws or the city leaders just don't give a shit. Looking at all of the ugly looking women and their grossly tattooed tits will make a straight man turn gay in short order.

If you still believe in the Rule of Law and Due Process then it would behoove you to read a very informative book entitled Kangaroo Justice And Well Dressed Thieves With A license To Steal. I have discovered that justice is in the eyes of the beholder and you will receive as much as you can afford. I consider the law and Due Process as just one big loop hole serving lying and crooked lawyers. If you think that Due Process for the innocent will result in a finding of not guilty then you're sadly mistaken. I'm a living example of how a lying lawyer and a kangaroo court can send an innocent person straight to hell. If you blindly accept Due Process and the Rule of Law as a prerequisite to receiving justice then you're living in a make believe world.

Whatever happened to national pride and the idea of supporting America? As I have pointed out before our so-called patriots are doing everything they can possibly do to destroy the American automobile industry. Look about when you're out for a drive and you'll see that 9 out of 10 vehicles on the road are foreign made. Every now and then some jerk will stick a decal of the American flag on the bumper of his Toyota to show his patriotism. Ignorance has no boundaries and if it continues our country will be pushed into a condition that grew in Germany prior to Adolph Hitler. History has a way of repeating itself and ignorance will only fuel the fire of national correction.

If a young man enlist in the military service he had better hope he's stationed in Iraq or some place in the Middle East where it's safe rather than within the United States where he could be killed. Worse yet become a police officer and see how long it takes before you get shot and assaulted. Having coffee, writing your report or directing traffic there's always some looney tune close by that will blow your brains out simply because you're a cop.

I'm not a prophet but I'm certainly not stupid either. When society has finally had enough a time will fall upon America that will be equal to the holocaust or worse. Plato's prophecy came true in post war Germany and so it will in America if we don't restore our country with the traditions that it was founded upon.

It just seems that my hard times will never end. In my twenty five years with law enforcement I've arrested lawyers for everything under the sun.

One was a prowler in residential neighborhoods and another one was arrested for attempted bribery. He offered me one hundred fifty dollars to throw a case against his client and instead I threw his ass in jail. If all of the crooked lawyers were arrested you'd have to build a dozen more jails to hold them. After years of law enforcement I finally came to the conclusion that most lawyers are nothing but well dressed thieves with a license to steal. A poor man like myself stands no chance of receiving justice standing alone in a courtroom. Please don't tell me about the Rule of Law, Due Process and Equal Justice under the law. Please spare me. I've experienced Kangaroo Justice first hand and know what the hell I'm talking about. Take it from me Due Process sucks big time and if you'd like to see how it can destroy you then read the book Kangaroo Justice by yours truly and see how the courts and lawyers can take everything you have like taking candy from a baby.

HARD TIMES

Have you ever been lonely in a crowded room? There was a period in my life that loneliness was eating me alive. Trying to raise my eight year old son after my divorce made me start thinking that I wasn't going to make it and survive, One day when I was really down I happened to meet a young lady that worked as a communications dispatcher with the Dade County Sheriff's Office. She pulled me out of a state of depression and the hopeless hole of despair that I was in.

The following is the exact note that I wrote one evening 47 years ago. Her name was Carole Ward at that time but I believe she has gotten married and her last name has been changed. As strange as it may seem she presently lives in Asheville, North Carolina just miles from my wife and I. Not one word has been changed and I entitled it "Myself."

Myself

One day my world suddenly crashed around me and I faced a mountain that I feared that I could not climb.

I felt that life had betrayed me and the end result of everything was a lie. That unbreakable silver thread of faith that held my life together and that I held onto so tightly and dearly was suddenly cut before my eyes.

The beautiful warm sunlight of day failed to warm me and the enchantment of night only served me with more loneliness. No longer was I able to see the beautiful creations about me or to smell the fragrance of my roses.

The love in my heart was quickly dying against my very will. For my mind had been robbed of my most precious possession…peace.

My presence was here but my feelings, emotions and dreams I locked deep within myself so no one could ever hurt them again.

Time became of no importance and my happiness or sorrow I measured one day at a time. I fought against the memories of yesterday and could not dream of tomorrow. My existence was just for today.

I live to harm no one and ask only the same from my fellow man and when I die and pass through death's door, let no man say that I ever placed anything in his path of life.

I became an island unto myself, one which life created for me because of my human weaknesses. Against my will, I remain a prisoner of myself. My heart cries out for love but the past seems to be my master and refused to permit entry onto my island.

At times I fear that all of my tomorrows will be shadowed by yesterday and doubt if I will ever have the capacity to change it.

My existence has grown to a great degree of insignificance and I am constantly reminded of how unimportant I really am to anyone other than myself.

I strive to understand myself but the answers and reasons elude me endlessly. I feel that I stand alone to face life on my own ground and terms, afraid to venture too far.

You gave your friendship to me and never asked for anything in return and I soon realized that I had even unknowingly eliminated trust and friendship from my life.

I found myself admiring your philosophy of life and like a thief and without your knowledge I began to steal your very thoughts because in them I found comfort.

HARD TIMES

Whatever life offers me I don't know but one thing for certain, your friendship has seemingly penetrated that protective shield that I so carefully wrapped myself in.

When you talk and a smile comes upon my face it's only a reflection of my gratitude and sincere feelings and certainly for no other reason.

I feel very thankful that I met you and will always keep your friendship and our memories in that little secret corner of my heart.

The End

To this day many years later I still have her in that little secret corner of my heart. She is truly a good person and I'll never forget what she did for me and made me realize how much happiness can be in life. She gave real meaning to friendship and what it means.

Good things will always come to an end sooner or later. That's a rule that applies to a person and a nation. Don't waste your time looking back at what could have been because nothing can change the past.

It's been said that if people don't recognize the past then they are doomed to relive it. For myself I'm totally convinced that lawyers are the ruination of our country. Right now our country is being invaded by illegal immigrants by the millions and the Democratic leadership do nothing about it. We have money seeking lawyers crawling all over each other meeting the immigrants and telling them how to beat the immigration laws. It's high time for the country loving patriots to start kicking some ass because that's the only thing stupid people can understand.

The lawyers have found a gold mine in representing the immigrants and couldn't careless what kind of background they may have as long as they have money. Their so-called asylum claims are nothing but a lot of bullshit and everyone knows it. They have no doubt heard that everything in America is free and they want some of it. All of the assholes running for president on the Democratic ticket are seeing who can give away the most for votes. One flaming asshole wants to give every person 18 years old and over $1,000.00 a month. Looking at all of the candidates it's amazing to see that all of them appear to be assholes.

All of the trash passing through Mexico to get to America cancels their pissy ass claims for asylum in America. When you're standing in a free country asking for asylum in another country then you're pissing in the wind. Of course that doesn't make any difference to a lawyer. Screw the legalities, we'll worry about that later just give me some money. When there's a way of making a dollar then the American law can go to hell.

Looking at and hearing the candidates that are running for president on the Democratic ticket will give anyone a severe case of irritable bowel syndrome. Our country certainly does face a crisis and it's all of the brainless assholes running the Democratic Party. They offer the country nothing and run around in circles not knowing whether to shit or go blind. They're so busy kissing each others ass they don't have any idea what's going on. I've seen a truck load of ignorance in my life time but nothing to equal that of the Senate Majority Leader and the Speaker of The House. They spend most of their time scratching their ass and trying to figure out a way to obstruct President Trump. They finally decided that if you can't win an election then change the rules. Now we have Democrats that have their brains in their underwear trying to do away with the Electoral College. What the Democratic Party stood for years ago simply doesn't exist anymore. As insane as it sounds they are now objecting to anyone having to say that they're a citizen of the United States on a census form. There's absolutely no limit to what the assholes will object to.

HARD TIMES

What really bothers me is to see forest fires and floods because I know that the poor animals and wild life are going to get killed. As far as I'm concerned let California burn to the ground because the people in California deserve what they get for supporting and voting for such assholes as their governor and representatives in Washington. The governor made California a sanctuary state to hide and protect criminals from the law. They have thousands of homeless bums sleeping in tents along the main boulevard and the sidewalks are covered with feces and urine. Some of their cities are nothing but a toilet for every bum in town. It's almost impossible to walk down the sidewalk without stepping into piles of shit.

I'm going to tell you a story and if I'm lying I hope the Lord strikes me dead. I went into a large department store and was shopping on the second floor which was crowded with shoppers. I was standing within twenty feet of a large concrete pot holding a small palm tree when a Mexican appearing fellow walked up to the pot, pulled his pants down, sat on the edge of the pot and shit. When he finished he got up, pulled his pants up and casually Walked off. By his behavior and the way he looked so relaxed I'm sure he didn't think that he was doing anything wrong. I guess I should be thankful that he didn't shit on the hood of my car or on my front porch at home.

Some people can get over being ripped off and screwed but I'm not one of those people. In 2016 I had a couple brainless lawyers and a potted plant judge stick it up my ass without requiring any evidence that I had done anything wrong. Every now and then I write the judge a nice letter asking him if he has ever figured out a way of justifying his ruling against me denying me the protection of the state law "tenants by the entirety." As of yet he has never shown me the courtesy of a reply but that doesn't surprise me because he never even recognized that my wife and I were in the courtroom during the hearing. The young lawyer trying to present a case against me couldn't produce one document or one iota of evidence to prove his argument and even at that the judge (using the term loosely) ruled against me opening the door for anyone to plunder and steal everything I owned. Without any justification he ruled that were "tenants in common" which denied me the protection of a state law.

There are probably a lot of people that still believe that lawyers don't lie under oath because they sign an oath that they will never misrepresent anything in a court of law. Folks, that's a lot of bullshit and if you still believe it then you had better take your head out of your ass and wake up to reality. Read the book Kangaroo Justice and see how easy it is to lose your ass after a simple minded lawyer gets finished lying about you. Things such as Rule of Law, Due Process, Equal Justice under the Law, Code of Silence, Privileged Communication and Innocent Until Proven Guilty is nothing but a crock of shit for the poor and ignorant to believe and live by.

One afternoon I walked by a lawyer's office and having nothing to do I walked in and asked a lawyer sitting at his desk doing nothing what it would cost to sue someone for slander. He stated that he charges $300.00 an hour and it would depend on how long the case would take. That was the extent of our conversation and being polite I asked him if I owed him for the information and without blinking an eye he responded that $75.00 would cover it. There my dear readers is an example of the law profession.

Everyone has their way of learning experiences in life. Some people may need help to learn something new but in my particular case I always taught myself. I learned to ride a bicycle by falling off and busting my young ass a half dozen times. I learned to swim by running from a farmer that was going to kick my ass for being in his watermelon patch. I learned to swim that afternoon by jumping into a close by river and swimming across for the first time in my life to avoid a good and well deserved ass kicking. As I have stated before I never had any money and I smoked crossvine and corn silk in place of cigarettes. Any young man that was growing up in the country and on a farm knows what I'm talking about. I lived and survived on the road of hard times and as the saying goes if you make a bed then sleep in it.

It seems like every kid that graduates from high school is bound and determined to go to college. As an adult male I've attended three or four different colleges and most of the young people I met in college weren't qualified to even be there and belonged in a vocational school learning a trade or in the military service. History shows that a large part of the college students never finish college and leave owing a student loan that they're still obligated to pay back to the government. Being in college will probably mean that you're going to be taught by some half witted liberal professor that doesn't know his ass from a hole in the ground. After four years of college you'll most likely graduate with the same level of intelligence as the half witted professor, not knowing your ass from a hole in the ground. Professors usually grow a beard because they think it makes them look more intelligent. It always amazes me that someone cultivates hair on their face that grows wild on my ass.

The Democratic Party sort of reminds me of myself in a way. When they get together they don't know what the hell is going on. It's the same way I feel when I'm having sex, I don't know if I'm coming or going. When I see and hear the Speaker of The House and the Minority Whip in the Senate I start thinking that they could use something else brain wise instead of a few votes. They don't support President Trump on anything that needs to be done for our country and as a matter of fact Mexico is doing more for our country than the Democratic Party. Too bad the Southern states lost the war for their independence. Every time I think of that war I'm reminded of the two people that got shot in the head. President Lincoln in Ford's Theater by John Wilkes Boothe and the guy sitting in front of Peewee Herman in an adult theater.

STORY

What ever happened to the good old days? When you could walk to the local store to buy a loaf of bread without the fear of being shot or mugged. When you could go to the department store, buy a television set, take it home plug it in and watch television without it costing you a dime. Today I pay $160.00 a month to be able to watch television which is basically commercials. When a hand shake was as good as a written contract. When a person's word meant something and was never broken. When being a patriot meant something like buying and driving American made vehicles instead of supporting foreign companies. When making America first wasn't considered a crime. As for me all of those foreign car owners that sticks a decal of the American flag on the bumper of their Nissan or Toyota to show their patriotism can stick the decal up their unpatriotic ass.

If anyones image belongs on Mount Rushmore, it's President Trump because not only did he Make America Great Again, he saved America from being destroyed by a radical Socialist Democratic Party hell bent on obstructing President Trump at every turn.

If someone ever started a legitimate movement to put his image on Mount Rushmore I'd be more than honored to donate $1,000.00 toward the project. Now we have some moron congress person introducing a bill to provide reparations to blacks for slavery two hundred years ago. This is an example of the ignorant mentality running rampant throughout the halls of congress. For myself if I was a black descendant from Africa I would thank God every day for slavery otherwise I would probably be living in squalor some place in Africa wondering where my next meal was coming from instead of driving a nice car and living in a nice air conditioned house watching television. That idiot in congress can stick her reparations bill up her fat ass. If she doesn't like what I've said then I'll bend over and she can kiss my Southern rebel ass along with that has been and washed up movie actor that supports her. Considering all of the flaming assholes running for president on the Democratic ticket if President Trump doesn't win I'll kiss the ass of the Democratic winner on the fifty yard line in the Super Bowl at half time. Does that tell you how confident I am that President Trump will win re-election in 20/20?

All you non-believers remember what I'm saying about the Obama Whitehouse and his involvement on the spying of President Trump including his campaign. With all the corruption in high places it would take an idiot to think that Obama didn't know anything about it. I just hope the hell I can live long enough to see all the crooked and sorry bastards go to jail. Like I've said before ignorance has no boundaries. I have people in my own family that doesn't know shit from shinola when it comes to judging character and recognizing the truth. It's high time for patriots to water the tree of liberty and the sooner the better.

Roe vs Wade and Planned Parenthood has murdered more human beings in the name of Women's Rights than Adolph Hitler ever dreamed of killing. There are actually people supporting infanticide and killing the baby after birth is quite acceptable. One jerk ass governor showed that he was compassionate and said that they would make the new born baby comfortable until the mother decided if she wanted it or not before they killed it. Maybe they plan on cutting the baby up and selling the parts like Planned Parenthood use to do or maybe still do as far as I know.

Politician lawyers have wrecked and destroyed too many lives to be walking around patting each other on the back. They have a society of their own and each one is programed to think they can do and say whatever they damn well please. The mayors and governors in our country will have to stand good someday for what they've done to our country by creating sanctuary cities and states to protect and hide criminals from law enforcement. Time and again they exhibit shit for brains as they stand proud of their chicken shit law degree. Every lawyer that I have ever dealt with has worn perjury on their sleeve as a badge of honor. They think nothing of lying under oath and misrepresenting facts in a court of law. Always bear in mind that approximately 84% of the people in congress are lawyers and that should tell you why our country is so screwed up and corrupt. The best thing going for President Trump is the fact that he's not a lawyer.

Be thankful for what you have because it can be taken from you when you least expect it. There are ten ways from Sunday that a lawyer can accuse you of something, lie about you and have you sleeping on the sidewalk with the rest of the bums before you know it. In my humble opinion that doesn't amount to much the ruination of our country is being caused by lawyers and their hunger for money. As in the case of O.J. Simpson, there's nothing they wouldn't resort to in order to get a double murderer found not guilty. Of course the jury consisted of nothing but racist morons who reeked of complete ignorance. Simpson's lawyers turned the concept of Equal Justice Under The Law into a laughable joke. As soon as Marci Clark and Darden walked into the courtroom and saw the make up of the jury they knew that the state's case was lost. Of course bear in mind that just because a person is found not guilty doesn't mean that he didn't commit the crime.

Being lost is the same feeling I had when I walked into the courtroom in Asheville, North Carolina when I was being sued by some trailer trash. Everyone that has ever been ripped off and robbed in a biased courtroom setting by a lying lawyer, please raise your hand and be counted. If anyone still believes in Due Process and Equal Justice Under The Law then you're living in fantasy land. The lawyers that robbed me represent the worse of society. Rest assured they couldn't careless if you're innocent of what you're being accused of. Their entire life is dedicated to finding someone to sue and guilt or innocence has nothing to do with it. Go to a disaster involving life and property and you'll probably get trampled by lawyers running all over the place signing up clients. Try and believe this. I had to pay a trailer trash couple $125,000.00 for producing and distributing hundreds of slanderous posters with my wife's picture all over the county including the front door of our church house for everyone to see Sunday morning. The trailer trash have been life long free loaders ripping off every welfare system they could find and the court had the gall and balls to reward them with my life savings.

If you want to see typical lawyers in action look at the morons running for president on the Democratic ticket. Apparently all of them are participating in a contest to see who can give away the most free stuff. The jerks are saying anything to make everything free to get votes. How does the government pay for it? Who cares just vote for me. Right now the polls show that the top three candidates are the has been Indian, the communist and the cock sucker. Unless things change that's the best the Democratic Party has to offer. You can't help but feel sorry for some of them. Take the case of Senator Biden, it's obvious that he doesn't know what the hell is going on or seeing anything because he's had his nose stuck in Obama's ass for eight years. He's another one like me when I'm having sex. He doesn't know if he's coming or going when he's in a debate.

The average college student probably doesn't belong in college because a lot of them don't know their ass from a hole in the ground. They usually want to go to a college out of town so they can run wild, get laid and get drunk on their ass without mommy and daddy knowing about it. Then we have piles of feces known as Antifa running around and taking every opportunity to assault any conservative that appears on campus. The city of Portland, Oregon is over run by this trash and the police just stand around doing nothing but scratching their ass while the Antifa thugs beat hell out of a journalist covering a demonstration. The Democratic mayor is apparently an asshole like his Antifa friends. Members of the Antifa mob are nothing but piles of dung that wear mask because they're too chicken shit to stand up like a man and be recognized for what they are.

It's a shame that the journalist didn't have a gun that he could have used to shoot the sorry bastards assaulting him. Then again maybe the police were too scared to do anything and found comfort sticking their finger up their ass. It's high time for the good people in America start eliminating the trash. Unfortunately most of the worthless trash belong to the Socialist Democratic Party which runs rampant throughout the Senate and House of Representatives. The present mob of Democrats seem to be completely worthless and follow the Speaker around like sheep.

We finally had a group of Democratic politicians go to the Southern border to see for themselves that a real crisis does in fact exist that they would never admit to. The trip seems to be a waste of time and money because one politician Cortez didn't know the difference between a toilet and a water fountain. The people that voted for that fruit cake must be as ignorant as her. I understand that her qualifications for being in congress was for dishing beans in some restaurant. At least that was more than Obama did before he was elected president. I've said it before and I'll keep saying it until hell freezes over. Retarded people and lawyers should be disqualified from holding public office then we wouldn't have half wits running all over the place shooting their mouth off about something that they don't know shit about.

The Democrats and liberals hate President Trump so much that if he farted they would form another committee and insist that the Environmental Protection Agency charge him with polluting the environment. They would insist that a special counsel be appointed to investigate the matter for a couple years to see if Russia had anything to do with it. With the Democrats it would be a simple case of high crimes and treason.

I love Independence Day and I always look forward to the 4th of July but sometimes my neighbors can really bug my ass. The neighbors around me start shooting off what sounds like sticks of dynamite

HARD TIMES

scaring the hell out of all the pets in the area. If they're trying to show patriotism then there's a better way of doing it. Buying American products like cars would be a good way to start. The same people shooting off the fireworks are the same people that are trying to put the American Automobile Industry out of business by buying foreign made vehicles. Let's face it those assholes don't give a rat's ass about supporting America. They're so busy thinking of themselves that it doesn't even occur to them what they're doing. I was born poor as hell and my personal vehicle is twenty three years old with 300 thousand miles on it which should tell you how well I'm doing financially. The way my life is going I'll most likely die poor as hell.

When Obama was running for president I had a friend that had a sticker on his Toyota that read "Anyone but Bush" which re-enforced my belief that he didn't understand what he was saying. I asked him to give me an example of what Bush had done that was so bad. He's a good man but it's obvious to me that his political beliefs are encouraged by his family. Considering what the Democratic Party has become I certainly wouldn't want people to know that I belonged to the party. History shows that the best Republicans are usually ex-Democrats.

Sometimes I wish I could just relive those good old days in the 50's and 60's. When you become an old person you live on the memories of the past and nothing pleases you as much as finding a long lost friend on the internet. As hard as I tried I could never locate my first love on the internet. Her name is Gail Ackerman and I carried her picture in my billfold for sixty years in vain. Rest assured and take my word for it. Getting old is not for sissies and it seems like you get smart when it's too late. I always tried to live my life by the "Serenity Prayer." Change the things that you can change and have enough wisdom to know the difference of the things you can't change. Living my life has not been easy and I've had my share of heart break and hard times. I'm just a simple and crippled old man that can't climb anymore mountains.

What ever you do in this life just be true to yourself. Set a goal and make it full speed ahead and you'll get there. Don't listen to nay sayers because most will only be jealous and offer no constructive help to you. Remember, your past is yours and belongs to no one else so be cautious of what and how much you tell anyone. In the twilight years of your life prepare yourself for pending death so that your family will be taken care of as best you can. I have already bought myself a burial site, funeral and headstone just to make sure I don't end up in a commercial dumpster behind Wal-Mart or someplace else. Most people don't like to think about final arrangements, Living Wills and etc. because it makes them feel uncomfortable. Every now and then my wife and I will go to the cemetery and decorate my grave site with flowers. As I stand there looking down at my decorated grave site it sort of gives me a new perspective on dying. We usually end up laughing and joking about it.

The one thing I'm guilty of is letting my health issues break my spirit. My beautiful doctor who I love very much gave me some advice on my last visit to her office. She said Robert, accept your physical problems and learn to live with them. Besides being a beautiful and compassionate doctor she's absolute right and I intend to do as she advised.

Sometimes I think I was better off living on that old broken down farm back in Alabama. The more I see of the boneheads in the big city the more I love animals. It has gotten to the point that America is in bad need of a revolution if we're going to survive as a nation that our founding fathers created. The U.S. Congress has grown into nothing but an old folks home for senile and mentally disabled people. Some radicals and freeloaders have been in Congress for most of their lives drawing big salaries for doing nothing but sitting on their worthless ass. Some of the blowhards have become multi millionaires which stirs the inquiring minds. The country is in desperate need of term limits in Congress but don't hold your breath waiting for all those assholes in Congress to do anything about it. They sure as hell won't do anything to spoil the gravy train that they've been on for years.

Now we have one moron running for president on the Socialist Democratic ticket that's been in Congress for going on fifty years. He's one of those misfits that has become a millionaire sucking ass and bull shitting the voters. Take a look at the line up of the idiots running for president and you'll fall out of your chair laughing your ass off. If that's not funny enough listen to them talk and you'll realize how totally ignorant they are. The top runner at present is a real package of bullshit. He really doesn't know what's been going on for the past eight years because of having his nose stuck in someone's ass.

It's just a simple fact that most people don't understand but you simply can't fix stupid. You can talk to a stupid person until you're blue in the face and regardless of what you say they'll still be stupid. It became obvious to me that stupidity has no boundaries. It runs rampant in large organizations and local government agencies. Have one bigot in any operation and it will do immeasurable harm which I have personally experienced on occasion. We have political people in the city, county, state and federal government that needs to be run out of town on a rail tarred and feathered. If I was a young man I'd be honored to welcome the opportunity to lead the charge against the scoundrels.

You can put it in the bank some day Plato's prediction will come to pass and there will be millions of citizens standing around scratching their ass wondering what happened. President Trump recently made a statement that I've been preaching on for the past couple years. As a matter of fact I wrote a book and published it entitled "America: Love It Or Get The Hell Out And From The Greatest Generation To

The Gutter Generation." I for one totally agree with what President Trump said, "If you don't like America then you can leave." Of course the flaming ass liberals and Democrats starting screaming that it was a racist statement. May I say, racist my ass. President Trump can fart and the Democrats will form a committee to have him impeached and demand that the Environmental Protection Agency file charges against him for polluting the atmosphere. If you want to see and hear total ignorance look to the so-called squad. Like I've said before it's common knowledge that stupid can't be fixed. The question of leaving applies to everyone in America that doesn't love America. I'm sure that the trash that decides to leave won't have any problem finding some shit hole country that they can live in and be happy.

During those trips down to the islands with Jeffery Epstein has changed Slick Willy to Nervous Willy. All it will take is for someone there to point a finger toward Slick Willy and hard times will be given a new definition. Nothing will surprise me anymore after having a twenty year old intern chewing on his crank in the oval office. That had to be one great tasting cigar. As the old saying goes some people have all the luck. Talk about things being confused the first lady was underneath the desk in the oval office taking care of business while the second lady was out walking the dog. That must have been one hell of a stain on that pretty blue velvet dress.

What I've said about book writing needs to be repeated again. It's a trip that will break you financially and leave you beating your head against the wall in frustration. Rest assured your book and effort will never be recognized unless of course you appear on Fox News to advertise it nationally. It seems like every author that appears on Fox News and advertises their book, the next day it's claimed to be New York Times best seller. It's quite impossible for an unknown author that has no name recognition to even get his book displayed in a book store much less get it advertised on national television. Just for example I contacted one nationally known radio talk show individual and he charges six thousand dollars a minute to advertise the book.

Most normal people have recognized that stupidity is an incurable brain disease that baffles medical science. It strangely shows itself mostly in so- called educated people that spent years in institutions of higher learning as in law schools. Apparently they become brain washed in the false belief that they are more intelligent than everyone else. They usually end up in a cesspool of ignorance like the United States Congress.

Let's make a few things perfectly clear. I'm not going to ever apologize for being white and if that bothers you then you can kiss my rebel white ass. It looks like we have one congress woman in the so-called squad of four that that couldn't out run her brother so she married him so the story goes. If it's true then no doubt she's a strong supporter of incest and keeping it in the family so to speak.

To this day I can't understand how a person can stand free in one country and apply for asylum in another country. It's obvious that the millions flooding illegally into our country breed like flies. Anyone selling condoms for a living in Mexico and Central American countries will starve to death because there doesn't seem to be a market for condoms.

Whether you like it or not business people in America caused the crisis at our Southern border by wanting cheap labor. The best vehicle that I have is a 23 year old truck with 300,000 miles on it. Yes, it pisses me off because I have yet to see a Mexican looking individual driving junk like I have to do. They seem to be partial to shiny new big trucks that I sure as hell can't afford to own. It's nothing to see a knocked up female carrying a baby in her arms and have two or three following her into an expensive restaurant to eat.

STORY

Our country's immigration laws are totally absurd and the program of getting knocked up in some other foreign country and then running to America to squirt out the baby so it can be an American citizen is nothing but a lot of bullshit. The Democratic Party and all of the assholes running for president on the Democratic ticket want to give the farm away. All of the jerks want everything to be free and will say anything to get votes. All of them support Socialism and poor old Joe ever since he pulled his nose out of Obama's ass he's been in a state of confusion and don't know what the hell is going on. I've witnessed severe cases of brown nose but he's given it new meaning.

Now that I look back on my life I see ways that I could have sat on my ass doing nothing like politicians making big money. Being a lawyer I could have legally stole people blind and ran for congress. I could have spent my entire life in congress stuffing the peoples money in my pockets. Look at how a lot of the people in congress have become multi millionaires. Doesn't it make you shiver to hear how many of them talk about and degrade our country? It's really sad because there's nothing we can do about it because you can't fix stupid.

My life has been one hardship after another through no fault of my own. The only explanation that I can offer is that I'm just an average poor slob that means nothing to anyone. Failure doesn't mean too much to me because it's been the way of my life. I've said it before and I'll say it again there are some people that should not be entitled to a trial. In my opinion serial killers should be drawn and quartered by four horses or fed alive feet first into a wood chipper so he can see himself being scattered into a hog pen as the hogs are eating him. Our present system will put them in prison for life and they become institutionalized. After becoming institutionalized you can't drag them out of jail and leave the good life where everything is provided for them.

HARD TIMES

As long as we live under the rules set by radicals in our society there will be nothing but chaos. Eventually Plato's prediction will become reality and the sooner the better. Ask a college student about Plato and they'll think you're talking about the cartoon character Pluto of Walt Disney.

When you get old you'll find yourself living on your memories especially your first love and those precious things that your mother taught you. Sayings like "Jesus loves me this I know because the Bible tells me so." The one that I've always been partial to and say every night is "Now I lay me down to sleep I pray the Lord my soul to keep, if I should die before I wake I pray the Lord my soul to take." I've always tried to live by the Golden Rule but sometimes I'm tested.

In 2016 I was flatly robbed of my life's savings of $125,000.00 by a lawyer and a "I don't give a shit judge" in Asheville, North Carolina. I have written to them numerous times in an effort to have them explain to me and justify why and how they could possibly rule against me without producing one document or one iota of evidence against me. Needless to say neither of them have ever shown me the courtesy of a reply. There's no way on God's earth that the court could find me doing anything wrong or violating any law. It's just an example of how a Kangaroo court can destroy a person with very little effort. That court created a mountain of hard times that I may never be able to climb. The destruction of my life was started by a dip shit female lawyer in Plantation, Florida who takes great pride in lying and filing false affidavits which are never refused by a circuit judge in Fort Lauderdale. That sorry lying bitch swore under oath that I "knowingly and willfully violated a court order" which was a lie that she admitted to me on two occasions. The judge was notified twice that she was filing an affidavit under perjury and he apparently didn't give a shit. The way she could lead him around by the nose I suspect that there was something between them if you get my drift.

If you find it hard to believe then read the book "Kangaroo Justice And Well Dressed Thieves With A License To Steal." If you're one of those people that still believe in Due Process and the Rule of Law, then by all means read the book and educate yourself. I'm an old man in bad health but hopefully I'll outlive that miserable lying whore. In her last name change the "a" to a "u" and it will describe her perfectly.

It seems like all you hear these days in Congress is the high national debt and the only thing they do about it is squawk. The way our government shovels out money to most of the countries on the planet in the name of foreign aid it aggravates the hell out of me. Half of the countries that get money from America hate America and that doesn't seem to make any difference to our government. As long as America continues to support more than half the world then stop bitching about the national debt.

All of the lawyers are in a frenzy running over each other trying to get their share of the big money involving the Roundup weed killing court case. Every time you turn on the television set you'll see two or three commercials from various law firms telling you to call them right away for a free consultation regarding suing Roundup because people are getting millions and you may not even have to appear in court. Call Grunt and Dump or anyone but call someone to get your share. One person was awarded two billion dollars but the court reduced it to 87 million which is still totally absurd. Ridiculous awards like that does nothing but encourage lawyers to file suits and destroy a company.

Recently the United States Attorney General William Barr signed an order to have five murdering scumbags executed that have been sitting on their ass for years being taken care of. Of course the usual loud mouth anti capital punishment crowds are running up and down the street screaming for the executions not to be carried out. The very people that are against the death penalty think nothing of supporting abortion and the killing of live unborn babies even to the point of infanticide. How the hell does it make any sense for a pregnant woman to object to the death penalty and then murder her own unborn child? I've said it before and I'll keep saying it until hell freezes over. When a woman is considering abortion she should be required to have to go to a Medical Examiner's Office and look at the perfectly formed little unborn babies floating and preserved in mason jars. If it pisses you off then so be it but abortion is simply another word for murder. Some day those people that kill their baby will have to stand before Almighty God and account for their actions. My heart cries out for little children and the thought of abortion hurts my very soul. God willing Roe vs. Wade will be reversed someday and the genocide of little babies will be stopped. Nothing in the entire world is more beautiful and rewarding then having a small child holding your hand or lying in bed beside you saying your name. You will discover that God made nothing stronger than the love you have for your child. I thank God every day for my children and the happiness that both have brought to me. Living in the twilight of your life and knowing that the time will come when it's time to go doesn't make it easy.

There's one other thing that should be addressed before I close out this book. It's an established medical fact that performing oral sex on females has given men throat cancer. For years medical science has been at a loss for the reason until now. The lawsuit against the weed killer Roundup is well known because every time you turn on the television set there are always three or four commercials from law firms telling everyone that has ever used Roundup to contact the law firm right away for a free consultation because it has been determined that Roundup causes cancer.

Now we have a lawsuit against Johnson and Johnson baby powder for the same reason and it is a direct cause of cervical cancer. It is common knowledge that some women have sprinkled the baby powder on their muff and in their panties for most of their life. Now it has been discovered that the baby powder has definitely caused cervical cancer beyond any doubt. That being the case it certainly doesn't take a rocket scientist to figure out why men are developing throat cancer from diving on a muff. No doubt throat cancer will be the cause of my demise because I've been diving on muffs ever since I was fourteen years old. I certainly don't ever expect to stop because the pleasure far out exceeds the danger. For me personally I can't think of a better way to go.

As I have mentioned before I will make a couple of points that people should understand before I close the book. First, people should understand what caused the massive influx of immigrants flooding into our country unchecked. Big business in their desire for cheap labor is solely responsible for the illegal immigrant crisis that our country faces today. Business owners knew that they could pocket millions by paying Mexicans and other people from Central America $3.00 an hour instead of paying American workers 12 to $15.00 an hour. The word got out and it wasn't long before thousands upon thousands of immigrants were crashing into our country whether we liked it or not. The only way it will stop is for the government to start placing heavy fines against the owners of the businesses and throwing their money grubbing assholes in jail. As long as the government refuses to prosecute the owners the crisis will continue. Fine the sons of bitches so much for each illegal worker that they will break out in a rash if one comes in wanting to be hired.

If you doubt what I'm saying then go on all the construction sites and see who is doing all the work. Go to a post office and see who it is making out all of the money orders to send back home to pay for the rest of their family members to come on over and enjoy the good life in America. The drug cartels find it more profitable to smuggle people to America then be bothered with the drug business. It's estimated that each person has to pay them from 6 to $8,000.00 per person to get to America. Apparently the immigrant problem is all over our country and the Democratic Party doesn't seem to give a tinkers damn about it. My wife and I have lost one eating establishment after another due to Spanish speaking people and Mexicans packing the place.

The second thing that I want to make perfectly clear so there's no misunderstanding is I will never apologize for being a white man and if there's someone that doesn't like it then they can kiss my lilly white Southern ass.

The last thing I'd like to suggest is directed to the American automobile industry. The Chrysler Corporation for example should come up with new and revolutionary ideas if they're going to stay in business. At present the patriotic American citizens are trying to put the American Automotive Industry out of business by buying foreign vehicles and not supporting American vehicles. The sad part is that the individuals buying foreign vehicles don't give a damn about the American Automobile Industry and it can go out of business for all they care.

Chrysler needs to take one of their pretty new pickup trucks, one without the extended cab and create a pickup/dump truck that will make every other pickup truck on the road obsolete. The new truck would appear as a regular pickup truck and all of the hydraulic lift equipment would be hidden and easily installed underneath the bed. It would revolution the never changing pickup truck into a vehicle that most every pickup truck owner would want.

In addition to the new truck the Chrysler Corporation should come out with a nice looking coupe with a rumble seat. Many years ago riding in the rumble seat was fault over by the younger generation. There wasn't anything more exciting then riding in the rumble seat going to football games, beach parties and special events or just riding around doing nothing. Either one of these suggestions would certainly appeal to the buying public far better than the Prowler vehicle. It would certainly behoove any one of the vehicle producers like Ford, Chrysler and General Motors to look into the suggestion and consider what it could do for their companies.

Letters regarding the suggestions that I have made will be sent out to all of the Chief Executive Officers of the mentioned companies in order to stir their imagination and how it could benefit their company. Innovation is the wellspring of any successful company. Hopefully one of the companies will at least consider the suggestions that I know will improve their operation.

There's one thing for sure, if President Trump loses the 20/20 election our country will be bound for hell. The Democratic front runner doesn't have both oars in the water and it's obvious that he doesn't know shit from shinola about China or any other country. All of the Democratic candidates seem to border on being a moron. It's hard to tell which one is the biggest jerk because each one has their own level of stupidity and like it says on the cover of the book "it's impossible to fix stupid."

THE END

www.ingramcontent.com/pod-product-compliance
Lightning Source LLC
Chambersburg PA
CBHW051946160426
43198CB00013B/2323